ADVANCE PRAISE FOR *RETHINK THE BINS*

"This well-researched guide clears up the many myths and mysteries of what happens to the nearly 8 pounds of trash we Americans create daily. The book answers the question, does recycling make a difference? Yes, but you must have the checklists here because they guide you toward actions that really do help the environment. Should be required reading in schools to help future generations embrace a circular economy."

—James Dillehay, author of *Start a Creative Recycling Side Hustle*

"If you're looking for a resource that demystifies what actually happens to the things we throw away, *Rethink the Bins* is for you! It's an easily digestible and interactive read. Goldstein's compelling writing style inspires hopefulness and action amid the often confusing task of reducing household waste."

—Moji Igun, Founder of Blue Daisi Consulting

"Finally, a book on waste reduction for realists! Julia demystifies compost and recycling, and her worksheets make this guide personal for you and your area."

—Summer Hanson, Co-owner of Eco Collective

"At a time when we're dumping mountains of food in landfills and filling the oceans with plastic trash, it's clear we need to change how we handle the problem of waste. *Rethink the Bins* is a great place to start: a clear, practical, and informative guide to the ways our waste systems work—and don't work. It's a valuable resource for anyone hoping to learn how to leave less trash behind."

—Susan Freinkel, author of *Plastic: A Toxic Love Story*

PRAISE FOR *MATERIAL VALUE*

"Meticulous editing and a succinct style.... Exemplary for its balanced and reasonable viewpoint, the text deserves to be classified as a reference tool for countless professionals."

—Publishers Weekly, BookLife Prize

"An engrossing, comprehensive overview of sustainable manufacturing and recycling and the challenges to expanding their adoption."

—Kirkus Reviews

"This book is an antidote to a world too dominated by extreme opinions: it is a detailed, balanced and fascinating account of how we can make the modern material world more sustainable."

—Mark Miodownik, author of *Stuff Matters* and *Liquid*

"A comprehensive, comprehensible guide to the impact of everyday materials like plastics and metals. If you want to take informed actions to support a better world, read this book."

—Anne Janzer, author of *Subscription Marketing* and *Writing to Be Understood*

"The clear explanations of the benefits and costs of so many types of modern materials, along with their current disposal methods, are valuable to anyone interested in moving our society toward a zero-waste future."

—Jill Lightner, author of *Scraps, Peels, and Stems: Recipes and Tips for Rethinking Food Waste at Home*

"In this compelling and informative book, you will learn about everything from chemicals and plastics to manufacturing and recycling, as well as what you can do as both a consumer and citizen to make for a more sustainable material world, all explained in a simple, clear, engaging style."

—David Biello, author of *The Unnatural World*

RETHINK THE BINS

RETHINK THE BINS

Your Guide to Smart Recycling and Less Household Waste

JULIA L F GOLDSTEIN, PhD

Bebo Press

**Rethink the Bins: Your Guide to Smart Recycling
and Less Household Waste**

The paperback edition of this book is printed on demand, eliminating the negative environmental impact of printing large quantities of books that might go unsold and contribute to waste. Organizations seeking discounts for bulk orders should contact the publisher.

Cover design: Michelle Fairbanks
Typesetting: Sue Balcer
Interior graphics: Sirajum Munir Galib
Editing: Ariel Hansen
Indexing: Judi Gibbs
Proofreading: Abbey Espinoza

ISBN: 978-0-9995956-4-0 (paperback)
ISBN: 978-0-9995956-5-7 (eBook)

Library of Congress Control Number (LCCN): 2020913332

TABLE OF CONTENTS

LIST OF ILLUSTRATIONS

LIST OF WORKSHEETS

My reusable plastic cup with
a Zentangle design

INTRODUCTION

THE MYSTERY OF THE MISSING CUP

I stepped away from the table for only a minute or two. When I returned, my laptop was still there, but my favorite reusable coffee cup had disappeared. I couldn't find it anywhere! How could I describe its unusual design to ask whether anyone had seen it? Then I remembered: I had written a blog post about this exact cup in a story touting the benefits of reusable plastic cups.

I pulled up my website on my phone and scrolled down the blog page to find the post, which included a photo of the cup. I spotted an employee (let's call her Jane) and held up my phone: "Have you seen this cup?"

She thought about it for a moment. "Yes. I threw it away."

It was an honest mistake. Jane was just trying to keep the area tidy, and my cup was empty. These reusable plastic cups from Starbucks are the exact shape and size of the paper cups, with an identical Starbucks logo on one side. The plain white reusable ones are hard to distinguish from the disposable variety.

But mine wasn't plain. It sported a design inspired from the practice of Zentangle, a meditative artistic expression that creates elaborate patterns in black and white. But apparently the design wasn't enough to convince Jane to leave the cup on the desk where I was working.

Jane and I walked over to the three bins in the kitchen area of this shared workspace and began searching. Success! Well, sort of. It wasn't in the trash. The cup was buried in the compost bin amongst discarded coffee grounds and banana peels. The lid ended up in the recycling bin, which was filled with a mix of items that did not look recyclable: plastic forks, wrappers from energy bars, you name it.

After a trip through my dishwasher, my cup and lid were good to go.

But this story illustrates a problem that I see frequently. The presence of multiple discard bins confuses people. The different bins are designed to improve recycling and composting rates, but the lack of consistent labels makes everything harder than it needs to be. I see trash in compost bins and food waste in trash cans. Foil or plastic food wrappers don't belong with the compost or the recycling. If composting is available, apple cores shouldn't go in the trash. Recycling bins are often filled with a mix of recyclable containers and stuff that doesn't belong. My lid certainly did not, though lids from single-use coffee cups might be recyclable, depending on where you live. It is hard to know what to toss where, especially as best practices keep changing.

There are a lot of mixed messages out there.

Recycle everything you can!
Recycling does no good.
Don't throw that in the garbage; it's recyclable.
You can't recycle that; throw it in the trash!
Avoid plastic in any form.
Buy compostable plastic!
Always compost food waste.
Never put meat or fish in the compost.
Don't toss that there!

No wonder so many of us are confused about recycling and composting. Sometimes we feel like giving up trying to figure it out. We're worried that no matter what we do, it will be wrong.

HOW TO GET THE MOST FROM THIS BOOK

When I run smarter recycling workshops or talk to people about recycling, I find that almost everyone wants answers. People want to know what to do with specific items when they are at home or away. And, secondly, they want to know if their actions make a difference. To that second concern I say, yes, they do. You are only one person, but if you change your behavior and encourage those around you to change theirs, your influence is greater than you think.

This is an interactive workbook, filled not only with information about the various items and materials that make up the municipal waste stream, but with worksheets for you to complete, so you can track, control, and reduce your household waste. The options for access to the worksheets depend on the edition you are reading.

Print edition:
1. Write directly in the book or
2. Follow the URLs to download fillable PDF forms.

Kindle edition:
Follow the URLs to download fillable PDF forms.

PDF edition:
1. Type directly into the PDF or
2. Follow the live links if you need additional copies of any form.

The first three chapters will tell you what happens to your household waste after you toss it into a bin. Feel free to read the chapters in detail or skip to the end of each chapter where I summarize the key takeaways.

Chapter 1 provides background on the state of recycling and composting in the US. I recognize that the US is not the only country that can benefit from a better understanding of how to handle household waste. But it is beyond the scope of this book to cover systems in Canada, Europe, or elsewhere in the world. If you are not in the US, I encourage you to research what systems are used where you live.

If you want to better understand what happens at recycling and composting facilities, read Chapters 2 and 3, respectively. Those chapters cover sorting and processing and should help you understand the intention behind existing policies.

If you want to know how to handle a specific category of material, such as paper, glass, or clothing, you may go directly to Chapter 4 where I group items into ten categories. Each category features an associated worksheet to mark which items apply to you and note what action they require.

Chapter 5 proposes three ways to track your monthly waste stream and suggests methods you can use to reduce the amount of waste you generate. It contains multiple worksheets to direct your tracking and guide you to discovering strategies that will work for you.

If you would like to see an example of how this works in practice, I tracked my family's waste for a month. I share the results, along with a list of useful resources, in the Resources section beginning on page 103.

GLOSSARY

Before diving in, it will be helpful to clarify a few terms. I'm listing these alphabetically rather than in order of importance.

Curbside: Americans living in single-family homes in many urban or suburban communities are familiar with the colored bins on wheels that waste-hauling companies provide for sorting household waste. Residents bring these bins to the curb for pickup. Residents of multi-family dwellings often have large dumpsters instead single-household bins. If that's your situation, everywhere I mention curbside recycling, think of whatever collection container is available near your building.

Garbage: Any household waste that doesn't get recycled or composted is garbage. Even waste that should be recyclable often ends up as garbage.

Landfill: This is both a noun (a location where garbage gets sent to get buried forever) and a verb (the act of sending garbage to a landfill).

Recyclables: Recyclables are household waste that can be processed into new materials. As you'll see when you keep reading, just because something is recyclable doesn't mean that it will actually get recycled.

Trash: I use this term interchangeably with garbage. A garbage bin and a trash bin are, therefore, both the same. Whatever goes in there usually ends up in a landfill.

Waste: This term, which is short for municipal solid waste, comprises all types of household waste. It includes everything that gets landfilled, recycled, or composted.

When you're done reading this book and completing the worksheets, you should come away with an understanding of how to better manage your waste at home and away. I hope that you will feel more confident that the items you toss into recycling and compost bins are actually being recycled or composted.

You and the members of your household can create less trash and send fewer items to a landfill while ensuring that only items without a better destination go into the trash bin. If you are inspired to replicate this on a larger scale, you can request a policy change at your workplace, your favorite coffee shop, or in your community.

The global public health situation changed dramatically from the time I finished writing this book to when it was ready for publication. As a result, some of the suggestions in this book are not practical. Pick and choose those that make sense for you and your community, and consider the rest as inspiration.

I encourage you to send me a note at https://juliagoldsteinauthor. com/contact to share your feedback and results. I will be happy to feature your story in my blog to inspire more people to better control and manage waste. Here's to a less wasteful future and recycling that works!

CHAPTER 1

WHERE THE WASTE GOES

This book explains best practices and general guidelines for smarter recycling and waste reduction. I'm sorry to say, however, that this book alone will not give you all the answers about what to toss where. Rules and policies vary from city to city, even within one metropolitan area. Homeowners and apartment dwellers in the same community may need to take different actions. When you move, you will probably be faced with learning a new system even if the same company picks up your trash and recycling.

The examples throughout this book, primarily from the Seattle area where I live but also for other cities around the US, may or may not apply to you. Stay tuned, though, as I will explain how to look up current guidelines for your community.

US households are impressively wasteful. We generate an average of somewhere between 4.5 and 8 pounds of household waste per person per day. It's helpful to dig into national data to grasp the scope of household waste generation. But if you prefer to skip the data and just learn what happens to our stuff once the trucks haul it away, go to page 12.

The national picture. According to the US Environmental Protection Agency (EPA), Americans generated 268 million tons of municipal solid waste in 2017, the most recent year for which comprehensive data are available.[1] This equates to 4.5 pounds per person per day.

Per-person waste generation rates have been fairly constant in recent years, suggesting a total of 270 million tons generated nationwide in 2019 based on population growth.

These numbers, while large, are probably underestimating total waste generation. My calculations, based on the EPA data as well as information from Waste Management, Inc. and Republic Services, suggest that the total may be as high as 8 pounds per person per day. This is close to Edward Humes's estimate of 7.1 pounds in his book *Garbology*, published in 2012.[2]

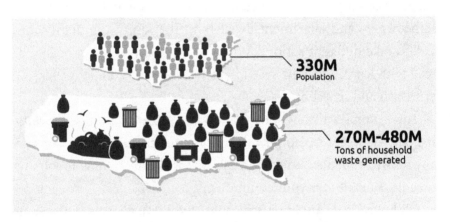

330M
Population

270M-480M
Tons of household
waste generated

Annual household waste generation
Millions of tons compared to the population of the US in millions. Based on 2019 estimates.

According to EPA data, paper and paper products comprise the largest proportion of waste (25% in 2017) and boast the largest recycling rate. Of 67 million tons of paper and paper products generated in 2017, 44 million tons (65%) were recycled.

How much is 67 million tons of paper? I weighed and measured a stack of magazines and did some calculations. A similar stack, if it weighed 67 million tons, would be around 240,000 miles high, equal to the distance between Earth and the moon!

The average US resident's contribution to that immense stack of paper is considerable. Assuming a population of 330 million people, we each accumulate a 38-foot-tall stack every year, or nearly five floor-to-ceiling stacks of paper. Whether landfilled or recycled, that's a lot of paper. No wonder we have a hard time decluttering! Fortunately, there are ways to reduce the amount of paper that comes into your home. It takes effort, but it is possible. I share some ideas in Chapters 4 and 5.

While paper waste has decreased since 2000 because of electronic documents, plastics represent a growing percentage of waste. Recycling rates for plastics are dismal, around 9% in 2015 and dropping. The Plastic Pollution Coalition estimated a plastics recycling rate of only 4.4% in 2018 and a prediction of 2.9% for 2019 because of the China effect (see page 10 on China's policy change).[3]

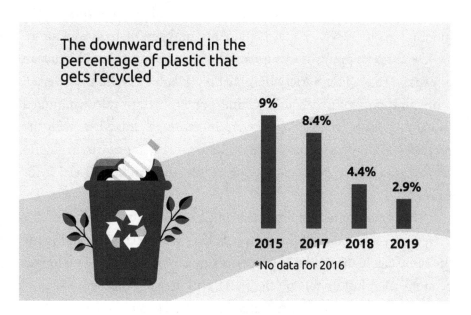

The downward trend in the percentage of plastic that gets recycled

9%   8.4%   4.4%   2.9%

2015   2017   2018   2019
*No data for 2016

After you learn what to do, the rules keep changing. Though they may seem arbitrary, there are good reasons for these differing and ever-changing rules, and it is important to modify your habits to keep up.

Local policies are based on:

➤ Available recycling and composting facilities

➤ Available methods to process waste

➤ Laws at the state, county, or city level

➤ Cost of waste collection and processing

All the above policies continue to evolve. One big change that happened in 2018 was China's decision to stop buying trash and recyclables from North America and Europe, an abrupt reversal of nearly twenty years of standard practice. Since 2000, waste processors in the US had been sending increasing quantities of waste overseas (13 million tons in 2017), primarily to China, and getting paid well for it.

Overseas shipping of waste started with paper and metal but began to expand to a wider variety of mixed recyclables. As the US diverted more and more of its waste to China, contamination rates continued to climb—nonrecyclable items were increasingly mixed in with the recyclables. US processors could no longer make money by trying to recycle this highly contaminated mix, but they could still sell it for a profit.

At some point, waste importers in China must have evaluated the ever-decreasing value of the materials they were receiving, and made the same calculation the US processors had. The model was no longer economically sustainable on their end, and they put on the brakes.

Once China implemented this disruptive change, other countries in Asia soon followed its lead. As a result of these actions, the economics of waste processing suddenly shifted. Market prices dropped from around $90 per ton in early 2017 to $25 per ton by late 2019.[4]

In reaction, during 2018 and 2019, 54 communities in the US stopped curbside recycling completely, while others reduced the list of materials they would accept or increased collection fees. As of early 2020, many companies in waste management are still scrambling to adjust. Financial reports from the largest waste management companies show significant decreases in recycling revenue over that timeframe.

In the long run, China's refusal to buy low-value waste offers an opportunity for the US and other countries to step up domestic processing. Some of the largest companies, such as Waste Management, Inc. and Republic Services, have already been doing just that. Such actions can improve recycling rates and create new sources of recycled materials, as well as saving energy by not shipping waste overseas. Domestic processing also allows us to avoid burdening other countries with our trash.

The largest waste processing companies earn enough revenue from curbside collection that they can afford to absorb a significant reduction in recycling revenue in the short term. Smaller facilities don't always have that luxury. With processing costs around $80 per ton, businesses that don't make money from hauling waste—only from sorting or processing it—are struggling to stay afloat.

The burden of improving the system belongs to the waste management industry and to local governments. But as consumers, we can take steps to reduce the amount of waste we produce and properly handle our remaining waste. We can ask our cities to provide greater options for recycling. We can also ask our local waste management companies to provide clearer instructions and change their policies so that less material ends up in landfills. And we can ask the companies that make products we enjoy and depend on to use less packaging.

Some people insist that recycling is broken. I believe that throwing up our hands and saying that there's nothing we can do is not helpful. My advice instead is to educate ourselves and those around us and to promote practices that improve real recycling rates and reduce waste generation.

When waste is collected at the curbside, where does it go? The diagram below shows the options for various types of waste. The exact sequence can vary because not all services are available in all communities, but this will give you a basic idea of the possible steps.

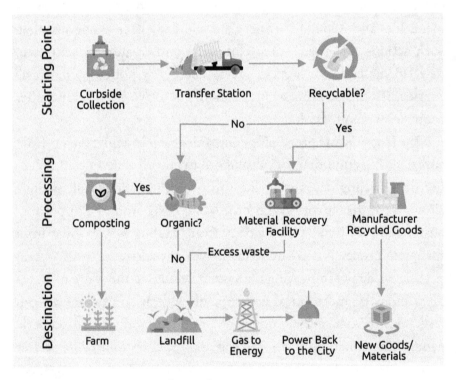

Where the waste goes
Possible paths from curbside collection to disposal or reuse.

Curbside collection typically includes three types of collection bins: garbage, recycling, and yard waste/organics. In this context, "organic" simply means plant- or animal-based waste. Think eggshells and orange peels, rather than inorganic materials like metals and plastics.

Some cities tell residents to separate out different types of recyclables for curbside collection, but single-stream recycling has become the norm (more on that in Chapter 2). Putting all types of recyclable materials into one bin simplifies collection. Contamination rates, though, are much higher with single-stream recycling than with multi-stream.

Waste deposited into a recycling bin heads to a material recovery facility (or MRF, pronounced "murf") for sorting. MRFs usually send paper, plastic, metal, and glass to separate processing plants that grind or shred them and process them into recycled materials. Material that is successfully recycled goes into producing goods with recycled content, while contaminated or otherwise nonrecyclable material heads to the landfill. Chapter 2 describes more about what happens at MRFs and processing plants.

In an ideal world, all waste would either be recycled into new goods and materials, turned into compost, or burned to generate electricity. Such a process is the heart of the circular economy, an economic model where almost nothing becomes waste. The circular economy stands in contrast to our existing, mostly linear, economy. The linear economy depends on products being created, used, and disposed of. It drives production of new materials and new goods and assumes that all economic growth is desirable.

In the circular economy, everything is part of either an organic cycle, where compostable materials return to the soil, or part of an inorganic cycle, where materials like plastics, glass, and metals are recovered to make new products. If you want to learn more about the circular economy, the Ellen MacArthur Foundation (see page 107 in the Resources section) has been instrumental in promoting the concept.

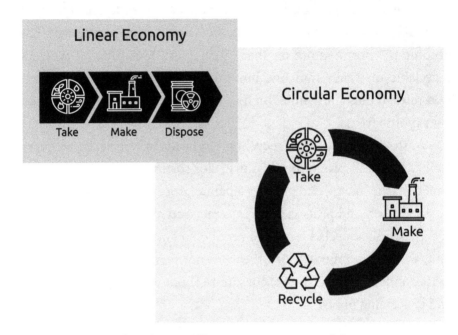

Circular and linear economy models

Moving to a completely circular economy is an ambitious goal. In reality, much of our waste heads to landfills where it takes up space and provides no real value. Are landfills reaching capacity? While hundreds of landfills around the country have closed, remaining capacity is enough to last hundreds of years. The issue is the location of landfills and the distance that garbage must travel to reach them. For example, no municipal landfills remain open near New York City. Trash there goes to landfills out of state, more than 100 miles away. Trash from Seattle travels even further, to a landfill in northeastern Oregon. At least it is transported by train rather than by truck, reducing the impact of emissions from the 260-mile trip.

But the main problem with landfills isn't capacity or location. There are more pressing concerns, such as the economic value of the items discarded into landfills. If diverted properly, the items now being discarded can produce new raw materials or energy worth billions of dollars per year. Many discarded items, such as clothing, furniture, and electronics, are still usable. Some are high enough quality to be worth selling as secondhand goods, while others can be repaired or refurbished and sold.

Landfills also pollute air and water. Although plastic liners in landfills contain much of the liquid that collects from wet garbage and rainwater, the liners can leak, releasing contaminants into the ground. Studies of drinking water near landfills have shown the presence of toxic chemicals.[5]

Another problem is the emission of methane and other greenhouse gases (GHG) into the atmosphere from landfills.

In 2017, landfills in the US emitted 108 million metric tons of CO_2 equivalent.[6] To put this number into perspective, it's about the same as annual CO_2 emissions from energy consumption (electricity, heating, and transportation) for the entire state of Alabama.

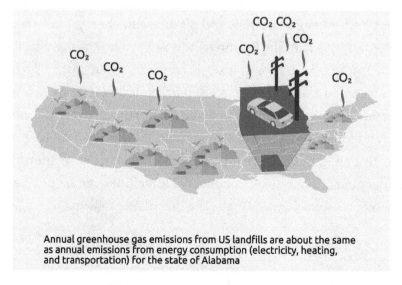

Annual greenhouse gas emissions from US landfills are about the same as annual emissions from energy consumption (electricity, heating, and transportation) for the state of Alabama

There are two ways to reduce GHG emissions from landfills:

1. Send less material to landfill. This goal can be achieved by reducing the amount of waste generated, increasing recycling and composting rates, and burning waste for energy.

2. Capture methane from landfills and convert it to energy.

Reduce waste generation. Of the ways to send less waste to landfill, reducing how much we create in the first place is the best option. Given the challenge of convincing businesses and individuals to control consumption, however, that strategy alone will not be enough.

Diverting organics, especially food waste, to composting facilities, represents a huge opportunity for reducing the associated GHG emissions. More than 200 landfills in the US are located within a mile of composting facilities.[7] But few composting facilities accept food waste. As a result, neither do most curbside collection systems. On the bright side, the availability of composting for yard trimmings has increased substantially during the 21st century. Yard trimmings are now much more likely to head to composting facilities than to landfills.

Burn waste for energy. Waste-to-energy (WTE) plants can convert both organic materials and plastics into energy. They serve as an alternative to landfills for mixed waste. Very few of these facilities operate in the US because of historic concerns about cost and release of toxins. Those are, for the most part, unfounded fears, as WTE plants burn the waste in a controlled manner that safely captures odors and toxic fumes. Industrial manufacturing poses a much greater threat to public health, but the public isn't clamoring to shut down manufacturers. If the costs to build WTE facilities can be justified, it could be a reasonable way to mitigate the waste problem.

WTE is much more popular in Europe, where landfill space is more limited. Manufacturing companies that boast zero waste to landfill tend to rely on WTE for a significant part of their strategy. That said, WTE should not be a justification to ignore the need to reduce waste generation and improve recycling practices.

Capture methane from landfills. Methane capture is something worth pursuing. The Landfill Methane Outreach Program (LMOP), run by the US EPA, tracks data from more than 2,600 landfills in all fifty states plus Puerto Rico and the US Virgin Islands. More than 1,200 landfills in the LMOP database operate landfill gas collection systems that convert methane into energy in the form of natural gas. The US government is looking to expand this program and has identified hundreds of sites where they can install methane capture technology. Methane capture does not collect 100% of the methane in landfills, but it still helps.

Looking at global emissions. Project Drawdown, a nonprofit organization that assesses methods of reducing GHG, evaluated the impact of various global changes on total CO_2 emissions. The organization considered strategies ranging from changing our diet to investing in renewable energy. Some of the results are surprising. The action responsible for the greatest reduction was proper handling of chemical refrigerants used in refrigerators and air conditioning units when these appliances are discarded.[8] The infographic on the next page shows the impact of the top five actions, along with capturing the power of waste.

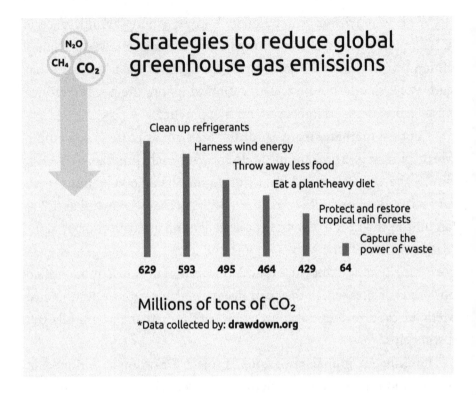

Strategies to reduce global greenhouse gas emissions

Clean up refrigerants

Harness wind energy

Throw away less food

Eat a plant-heavy diet

Protect and restore tropical rain forests

Capture the power of waste

629   593   495   464   429   64

Millions of tons of CO_2
*Data collected by: **drawdown.org**

From an energy perspective, increasing the use of wind power is much more effective than building more WTE plants, but that doesn't mean that WTE isn't a helpful strategy. Food waste is a significant part of the problem, and composting can help reduce it.

The role of recycling. Increasing rates of recycling, one of the strategies I highlight in this book, can reduce the amount of waste going to landfills. I don't propose that better recycling is the answer to the global problems of climate change, ocean plastics, and pollution. Recycling is far from a panacea, and there are other strategies that will make a greater difference.

But I do see smarter recycling as one step toward a less wasteful future. Ideally, society should move away from disposable packaging and the need to figure out where to toss it. The tide is turning, and companies are seeing customer demand for solutions that use less packaging, which is great. Customers also want less frustrating packaging. We can all do without sealed blister packs that are hard to open or packaging with labels that contaminate recyclables.

I also endorse an attitude of thinking before buying, be that necessities or luxuries. The goal should be to buy less and consider each purchase more carefully. Will you use and enjoy the product? Or will it spoil before you can consume it, or take up storage space without serving its intended purpose?

One aspect of the circular economy is product design. Products that are designed to last longer or be repairable help reduce waste, as do those made with recycled or recyclable materials. Such products are often more expensive for the initial purchase, but the total cost of ownership must factor in the extra months or years of useful product life. A $150 pair of shoes that lasts ten years is a much better value than a $30 pair that falls apart after six months of wear.

But I'm a realist. I realize that asking everyone to restrict their purchasing and carefully consider the carbon footprint of everything they buy is a tall order.

Until society embraces a fully circular economy, recycling matters. Items that are recyclable should be recycled. Making an informed decision before tossing something into the trash or recycling bins will allow recycling to work better. If contamination rates at MRFs in the US held to 5% or lower, the economics of recycling could work. Clean streams of recyclables—metals, specific plastics, dry paper, or glass bottles—can be processed into new materials.

Unfortunately, curbside recycling programs in the US are hardly collecting clean streams. According to a 2020 report from The Recycling Partnership, the average contamination rate is 17%, meaning that for every 100 pounds collected, 17 pounds are stuff that doesn't belong.

And that's for the communities that report contamination rates. The two-thirds that don't could have rates that are much higher.[9]

The cleaner the stream, the lower the cost to process it and the more potential applications exist for reuse. Materials in clean streams carry the possibility of recycling into the same types of products or even upcycling, where they are recycled into higher-value durable products.

Any type of improvement in waste processing requires effort. It's easier to toss everything into the trash, like we used to do before curbside recycling existed and what communities without recycling services still do. When recycling is available, it's easy to toss everything that might be recyclable into the big blue recycling bin.

When you understand the reasons behind your city's recycling rules, you are more likely to think about whether that empty container in your hand will end up in a landfill. If I can convince more citizens of the importance of a certain level of sorting and cleaning, it will help build awareness as well as increasing the value of recycled material. And if I can inspire citizens to reduce the amount of waste of all types that they generate, that's even better.

KEY TAKEAWAYS

➤ Rules and policies for recycling and composting vary from city to city even within one metropolitan area. Even once you learn what to do, the rules keep changing.

➤ Three strategies can reduce the amount of waste going to landfills: less waste generation, higher recycling and composting rates, and burning waste for energy. Individuals can easily help with the first two.

➤ Until society embraces a fully circular economy where nothing goes to waste, recycling practices matter.

➤ Contaminants like food residue and nonrecyclable packaging reduce the value of the stuff in our recycling bins and the likelihood that it will actually get recycled.

➤ The cleaner the recycling stream, the lower the cost to process it, and the more potential applications for reuse.

CHAPTER 2

UNDERSTANDING RECYCLING

When the items from recycling bins enter the material recovery facility (MRF), they go through several stages of sorting. The level of sorting required depends on whether curbside collection is single stream, where residents dump everything into a single large bin, or multi-stream, where residents presort their recyclables into two or more categories. Multi-stream systems separate paper from all other materials and may also require additional sorting.

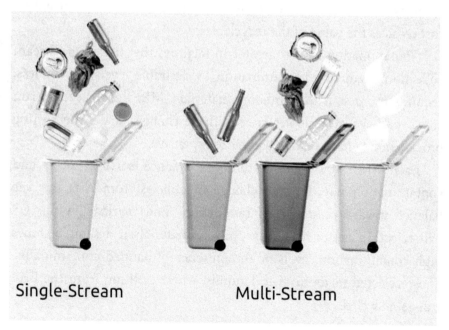

Single-Stream   Multi-Stream

Curbside recycling options

The single-stream approach increases participation, which is part of why many cities have migrated to this type of collection. It's easier for residents to choose among two options (trash or recycling) than to figure out which of many recycling bins to use. Single-stream recycling also allows for trucks with one large compartment. The truck can be filled to capacity before unloading at the MRF. Trucks with multiple compartments may need to unload their waste when only one of the compartments is full, leading to less efficient routes and more fuel consumption.

But easier recycling comes at the expense of a less efficient process once the materials reach the MRF. More machines are required to separate out the various materials. It takes energy to run these machines. It also takes time, both to run the machines and to remove items by hand that don't belong in the recycling stream. The resulting cost reduces the value of the recyclables.

Contamination is also greater in facilities that use single-stream collection. Reducing contamination to desirable levels, 5% or less, requires more staff to hand-sort materials. MRFs also need to run conveyor belts at a slower speed. These changes make the sorting process more effective, but also more expensive.

Each MRF must decide how to balance sorting speed and contamination rate, but the change in policies from Asia tips the balance toward reducing contamination. End markets in the US will reject an entire load of recyclable materials if a sample shows high contamination levels or the presence of banned contaminants. These rejected loads head to landfills, where nothing from the load will get recycled.

SORTING AND PROCESSING DIFFERENT MATERIALS

Once materials arrive at the MRF, they go through the following basic steps:

1. Trucks dump materials into a holding area.

2. Materials move onto feeders and conveyor belts.

3. Staff hand-sort to remove plastic bags and large items that will jam the sorting equipment. These items go either to a facility that can process them or to a landfill.

4. Materials are separated into categories: paper, cardboard, plastic, glass, ferrous metals (iron and steel), aluminum, etc. A variety of equipment automates the sorting process.

5. Each stream of materials is sent for further processing, usually at a separate facility. The paper and plastic streams are compacted into bales—large rectangular blocks—before shipping to a processor.

Making a bale of collected items into raw materials that qualify as recycled content involves multiple steps that are specific to the type of material. The cleaner the input, the more efficient the process and the lower the cost per ton of material received.

The following sections explain what happens to common materials at the MRF and how they get recycled once they move to the next stage at a processing facility. Once you're done reading this chapter and see how sorting and processing works, you will better understand why curbside recycling programs accept or don't accept specific types of packaging.

➤ Paper

Bales of paper go to paper mills for recycling. Paper recycling is a multi-step process that consumes energy and water, but making recycled paper is still less resource-intensive than making virgin paper from trees. The bales are separated by grade or quality. The length of fibers determines whether the paper is suitable for recycling into printer paper, lower grade newsprint, or other categories of paper products. The more times paper is recycled, the shorter the fibers get. Eventually, the material is no longer good for recycling into new paper.

Sorted paper gets shredded into small pieces and then mixed with water and various chemicals to break down the fibers and make pulp. The pulp is pressed through a screen to remove contaminants including metal, plastic, and adhesives. Because of this cleaning process, papers that are stapled together or envelopes with plastic windows are recyclable. The cleaning can't, however, remove food, especially greasy residue like that from pizza boxes. That's why you should keep that greasy paper or cardboard food container out of the recycling bin.

Once the paper pulp is cleaned, it is dried and formed into rolls of recycled paper ready to be made into new products. Recycled pulp is sometimes mixed with virgin pulp to improve the properties of the recycled paper. You've probably seen paper with 30% recycled content in office supply stores.

➤ Metals

Metals are one of the easiest categories of materials to sort and recycle. Magnets can easily pull out ferrous metals like iron and steel since they are magnetic. Other specialized machines separate out anything that is electrically conductive, easily extracting metals from plastics and other nonmetals.

Separating out metals is cost-effective because metals have a relatively high dollar value per pound. Recycled metals have the same properties (strength, hardness, etc.) as virgin metals but take far less energy to produce.

Metal can be recycled many times into bars or ingots that are indistinguishable from virgin metal. Structural metals like steel and aluminum are widely recycled. They can be melted and purified in a process that takes much less energy per ton of metal recovered than mining metallic ores and extracting the metal within them. Recycling the two dozen metals inside cell phones and computers is more difficult, but e-waste processing can recover gold and many other valuable metals from electronics.

At e-waste processing facilities, the economics are in gold's favor. The high resale price easily justifies the expense of extracting it from used electronic devices. And electronic devices also contain silver, aluminum, copper, and many other metals. Recovering these metals from e-waste reduces the need for mining, which is dangerous to workers and damages the environment. If e-waste recycling rates increase and processing becomes more efficient, the market for other recovered metals will grow.

Plastics

Plastic recycling is much more complicated than metal recycling. Plastics form a diverse waste stream made up of many dissimilar materials in various shapes and sizes. Plastics are often embedded in multilayer packaging that includes materials other than plastics. With a low value per pound, there's little motivation for MRFs to send plastics to recycling plants, especially when the end product is often inferior to virgin plastic. But some plastics are still worth recycling, and there are ways to improve recycling rates.

Plastic waste streams include a variety of materials that need to be separated from each other for further processing. A water bath can separate plastics that float and are less dense than water from those that are denser and sink, but it can't further sort the materials. This limit can be a problem since a single bottle of the wrong type of plastic can contaminate an entire batch.

MRFs often prefer to sort plastics by appearance. These shape-sorting systems are used for plastics that meet three criteria:

1. Science: the material itself is recyclable,

2. Technology: the sorting machine can separate it from the rest of the items in the recycling stream, and

3. Economics: an end market exists for reselling the plastic.

Plastic bottles, jugs, and tubs typically meet all three criteria. Sorting plastics by shape can help separate the different types so that, for example, water bottles go into one stream while milk jugs go into another. If your local recycler sorts by shape, please don't crush or squash the plastics to get more items to fit into your recycling bin. The automatic equipment needs the items to be intact to identify them.

Plastic grocery bags and lightweight plastic films are made from a recyclable material, but they fail the technology test. These items are incompatible with most recycling systems because they get caught in the gears. For this reason, bagging up mixed recyclables into plastic bags and putting them into the blue bin is usually a bad idea. It is best to let everything remain loose unless your city specifically directs you to bag items together.

I toured my local MRF, a facility owned by Waste Management, Inc. According to the tour leader, plastic bags are the mostly commonly seen contaminant in the recycling stream. Workers remove loose bags or large bags full of recyclables by hand early in the sorting process. These bags might go elsewhere for proper sorting and processing or they might be sent to a landfill where the recyclable items will never get recycled. But the conveyor belt moves fast, and hand-sorting doesn't catch everything. The tour leader told us that the facility must shut down their equipment several times every day because of clogs from plastic bags.

For more information on which plastics belong in curbside recycling, see page 56 or check with your local provider. As systems are upgraded or markets for recycled materials change, policies change accordingly, but these are some common best practices.

What happens after plastics get compressed into bales for processing? They go through either chemical or mechanical recycling, depending on the material and the technology available. Mechanical recycling, which is the most common method, breaks the plastic into tiny pieces and then melts it. Mechanical recycling retains the highest amount of the material's value. This is especially true for closed-loop recycling, in which a material is recycled into the same type of object. For example, used water bottles made from polyethylene terephthalate (PET) get recycled to make new PET bottles.

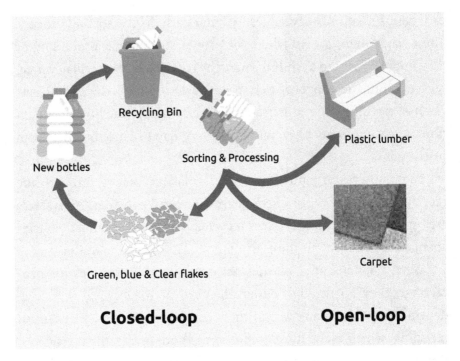

Recycling of PET water bottles

PET water bottles are the most successfully recycled type of plastic packaging, with a recycling rate of around 25%. Using recycled PET rather than virgin PET reduces the energy required to produce bottles by 60–80%. Companies are developing processes that can recycle PET bottles of any color mixed together, but the standard process recycles only clear bottles.

The presence of contaminants can make the recycling process less efficient and more expensive. Contaminants may include other plastic materials, food and beverage residue, and pigments. The standards are strict: Batches of PET with more than 100 parts per million (0.01%) of foreign particles get rejected. Improved sorting and cleaning processes can help to minimize the amount of contamination and improve recycling rates.

In open-loop recycling, the material that is ground up is used in a lower value application. A PET bottle, for example, would then be turned into carpet fibers or plastic lumber. This allows bales with higher contamination levels to find new uses in products that will last for many years, even decades. These types of materials cannot be economically recycled again, however, so once the carpet or lumber is discarded, it heads to the landfill.

Both closed-loop and open-loop recycling of PET bottles involve mechanical recycling. Chemical recycling is less common. This method breaks down the polymer molecules in plastics into individual monomers (the small molecules from which the polymers were originally made). Monomers recovered during chemical recycling substitute directly for the same monomers derived from fossil fuel sources. The recovered monomers are chemically identical to conventional monomers, so they produce polymers of similar quality.

Today, very few plastics go through chemical recycling. For most plastics in household waste streams, chemical recycling is not realistic because of the high cost of the process and the difficulty of removing pigments and additives from common plastics. Several companies in Europe are working to improve the economics of chemical recycling and develop new processing methods, however, suggesting that its use will expand in the coming years.

Glass

Glass is best sorted out as early in the stream as possible to minimize contamination. Systems that use vibration allow lighter items like plastic to float away while glass bottles and fragments stay on the vibrating belt. Metal stays on the belt as well, but magnets can separate the steel before the glass is sent for further processing. Glass processing facilities can screen out nonmagnetic metals.

Some MRFs purposely break the glass into small pieces that will fall through a screen into a separate holding area. Small pieces of plastic can also fall through, which is why items like plastic lids less than a few inches in diameter shouldn't be placed into loose recycling.

MRFs with on-site glass cleaning systems benefit from receiving higher prices for their glass when they send it for processing. Communities with some level of sorting at the curbside, either dual-stream or separation of glass from the rest of recyclables, collect glass that is cleaner and therefore much more likely to get recycled into new bottles. Highly contaminated glass often isn't valuable enough to send for processing, so it ends up in a landfill.

MRFs must usually be located within 100 miles of a glass processing plant to make it cost-effective to send glass for processing. At processing plants, glass is separated by color using optical scanners and crushed into small pieces called cullet. The cullet then goes to glass manufacturers, where it is combined with raw materials and melted to make new glass. Glass with recycled content not only saves the resources required to process sand (silica) into virgin glass but allows the mixture to be melted at a low temperature, saving energy. Glass can be recycled over and over without loss of quality, unlike paper or many plastics.

Separation by color is important because each color (clear, green, and brown) has a different composition and melting point. Further cleaning to separate out metals and other contaminants also occurs before the glass is melted. Some glass gets ground into a fine powder for use in fiberglass insulation instead of entering the recycled glass bottle recycling stream.

Glass that is too contaminated to sell to a processor can sometimes find other applications. These include fillers added to cement for building roads. Even glass sent to landfills can be of use. If the glass is not dumped with the rest of the garbage, it often gets ground up to be used as daily cover for the landfills, suppressing odors and keeping out animals.

ALTERNATIVE RECYCLING PROGRAMS

When I learned that only about half of all Americans have access to automatic curbside recycling programs, I was surprised. I have lived my entire life in metropolitan areas on the West Coast, where curbside recycling has existed since the 1990s. But millions of residents in both rural communities and cities cannot drop their recyclables into a curbside bin. And, as I explained earlier in this chapter, many items made from recyclable materials cannot be easily recycled.

But there is encouraging news. Private businesses are springing up to pick up the slack and improve the outlook for recycling.

Several companies have developed programs to recycle items that don't belong in curbside recycling bins or provide service to communities without city-funded curbside recycling. The reality of the costs of recycling mean that these options are not free. They do, however, come with the convenience of at-home pickup or prepaid mailing of items. And sometimes manufacturers, not consumers, pay the cost.

Depending on where you live, you may have access to one or more of the following services. If you lack access, you can contact your city or county and ask them to consider expanding service options.

Recyclops

Recyclops (https://recyclops.com) targets communities in Arizona, Idaho, Oklahoma, Texas, and Utah where curbside recycling is not otherwise available. With the exception of Phoenix, where they serve apartment dwellers, Recyclops operates in rural communities. The program charges a monthly fee and accepts commonly recycled materials, but the allowed categories vary. Paper and plastic are accepted in all locations. Glass may or may not be allowed. In some locations, glass pickup is an option with an additional fee.

Recyclops provides customers with 13-gallon bags, which they are required to use. Rather than using standard garbage trucks, the company loads recyclables into pickup trucks for transport to MRFs.

Retrievr

Retrievr (https://retrievr.com) provides curbside collection of textiles and electronics. The free service is available on demand in select towns in New Jersey and Pennsylvania, but if you live outside the service area, you can mail in textiles and electronics for recycling. Collected items go to Retrievr's partners, which process them for reuse, refurbishment, or recycling, depending on the age and quality of the items. For electronics, Retrievr partners with R2 certified e-waste recyclers (for more about e-waste practices, go to page 60).

The company is actively recruiting more towns and cities to join the program and promote it to their residents. Retrievr also offers in-store bins for fashion brands to encourage the clothing stores' customers to recycle used or damaged clothing.

Ridwell, Inc.

Ridwell (https://ridwell.com) serves a limited number of neighborhoods in Seattle and surrounding cities. For a monthly fee, the company provides cloth bags for customers to deposit used batteries, light bulbs, plastic films, and textiles. The plastic films category includes grocery bags, baggies, bubble wrap, and other thin, stretchable plastics that do not belong in curbside recycling bins. Ridwell collects Styrofoam upon request for an additional fee. Their trucks come by every two weeks to pick up the items and leave the bags for refilling. The service is a convenient option, especially for urban apartment dwellers with limited storage space and lack of transportation to take items to a drop-off location.

All the items that Ridwell picks up are recyclable but not generally accepted in curbside bins because they aren't compatible with the sorting process and MRFs. For example, Seattle residents are not supposed to put plastic bags and films in the recycling. Most grocery stores in the area have bins designated for those plastics, or they can go in the Ridwell bin. These go to a central location where they get transformed into plastic lumber and similar products. Ridwell doesn't process the goods it collects but transports each type of item to an appropriate processing facility in the greater Seattle area. The company screens its partners to ensure that items get responsibly reused, refurbished, or recycled.

TerraCycle

TerraCycle (https://www.terracycle.com/en-US) offers several programs for residential collection of hard-to-recycle items. They accept everything from toothpaste tubes to refrigerator water filters. The company disassembles items as needed into their various single-material components, which are then processed in a similar manner to other plastic, metal, paper, or glass waste streams.

Zero Waste Boxes allow residents to collect a wide range of household packaging and mail it back to TerraCycle for processing. This service is expensive, however, with a ten-gallon box costing just over $100. As a comparison, I pay $20 per month for curbside trash, recycling, and yard waste collection. It is certainly easier and less expensive to throw away stuff that can't be recycled curbside. But for those who can afford the cost and want more of their packaging recycled, the program is available throughout the US.

TerraCycle also works with durable goods companies to promote takeback programs. These partner programs are free to the consumer because the company that makes the product pays to have its packaging recycled. Each partner program collects a specific type of waste, such as foil energy bar wrappers or packaging from cosmetics, and they may only collect the sponsored product brand. The programs are not always available, however. When I attempted to sign up, I was placed on waitlists for some of them.

Loop, a TerraCycle company, delivers grocery, household, and personal care products in reusable containers. The products offered include a range of national brands. Customers return the empty containers, which get cleaned and refilled. The program charges customers a refundable container deposit. Products are delivered in a reusable tote with inner dividers to protect items during shipping. If Loop is available in your area and offers brands you already use, it sounds like a great idea. As of early 2020, availability is limited to specific zip codes in eight Eastern US states plus Washington, DC, and Paris, France, with plans to expand service to more communities.

Key Takeaways

➤ Single-stream curbside collection improves participation rates but increases contamination. It is too easy to dump everything into the big blue bin.

➤ Materials must meet three criteria to get recycled: made from a recyclable material, able to be identified and separated, and economically valuable enough to be worth processing into recycled content.

➤ Plastics are the most challenging type of material to recycle because of the many different types of plastics, low economic value, and high contamination rates.

➤ Glass recycling is limited by the high cost of transporting glass and the lack of available processing facilities.

➤ Open-loop recycling, in which disposable items are made into the same type of product, is ideal because the materials can undergo multiple cycles of reuse. Improved sorting and processing can increase implementation.

➤ Businesses are springing up to collect hard-to-recycle items and serve communities that lack access to automatic curbside recycling.

CHAPTER 3

UNDERSTANDING COMPOST

Compost is made from waste organic matter, typically a combination of yard trimmings and food waste, that would otherwise end up in a landfill. A properly designed compost bin breaks down organic matter within weeks or months into a nutrient-rich soil amendment. In contrast, organic waste sealed in a landfill can last decades without degrading. In *Garbology,* author Edward Humes tells the story of researchers excavating buckets of waste from a landfill. They discover identifiable avocado pulp along with old newspapers. The date on a newspaper is still legible, revealing that the avocado has been preserved in the landfill for twenty-five years![1]

When organic waste degrades in a landfill, it produces methane, a greenhouse gas more potent than carbon dioxide. Landfills are responsible for 18% of methane emissions in the US.[2] As I mentioned in Chapter 1, expanding composting is one way to reduce landfill-related GHG emissions. Instead of contributing to methane emissions, the organic waste is turned into a valuable commodity: compost. The amount of yard waste being landfilled in the US decreased considerably as municipal facilities began sending it for composting instead. According to US EPA data, the weight of yard trimmings composted in 2015 was almost five times the amount composted in 1990.[3]

THE VALUE OF COMPOST

Compost serves many beneficial purposes. Aside from the waste reduction benefit, compost is good for growing crops and reduces reliance on artificial fertilizers and pesticides. Replacing synthetic fertilizers with compost reduces air and water pollution. Compost also replenishes nutrients in the soil, improving plant health and increasing crop yield without the use of toxins.

Feeding gardens with compost is, of course, only one step in creating a healthier ecosystem where plants will grow well. Compost as fertilizer is most effective when combined with crop rotation and other best practices that are beyond the scope of this book. See the Resources section (page 106) for further reading about composting.

BACKYARD VS. INDUSTRIAL COMPOSTING

Not all composting methods are identical. In particular, industrial composting incorporates a level of control and sophistication that isn't possible in household or backyard composting. Backyard composting, however, is the best option for reducing transportation-related emissions. Organic waste that stays on your property and turns into compost that you use to grow flowers or food has no carbon footprint other than that associated with producing and shipping your compost bin. It's usually best practice to contain backyard compost where it is safe from animals and you can better control the moisture level by adding water as needed.

Industrial composting facilities process organic waste efficiently. They grind it up into small pieces that can degrade quickly and balance the composition of green matter (grass clippings, vegetable scraps, etc.) and brown matter (dried leaves, wood scraps, etc.) At some facilities, the compost is covered to maintain the temperature within a narrow window to speed up the composting process. Water and air are added or removed to keep the humidity at a desired level. Depending on the technology used, the process from organic waste to finished compost takes between eight weeks and six months.

Because of the processing equipment and methods available, industrial compost facilities can turn a greater variety of incoming organic matter into compost compared to what is possible in a backyard compost bin. Branches, leaves, and bones are ground up, as are compostable packaging items.

Most Americans don't have access to an industrial composting facility that accepts food waste. The state-of-the-art Sevier Solid Waste Composting Facility in Sevier County, Tennessee claims to be one of about a dozen such facilities in the US.[4] What a shame that there aren't more of these facilities, since Sevier County boasts that it diverts 70% of its waste from landfills. The county achieves this through both composting and recycling. Residents benefit by receiving free compost.

If you can't deposit your food waste into a curbside bin, you may have access to a community composting program where you can drop off containers of food waste. Cities and towns that run such programs can recover some of their operating costs by selling the finished compost.

Another option is to start a compost bin in your backyard or patio. The American Horticultural Society's Master Gardeners program, available in nearly every US state, can guide you to resources for everything from growing vegetables to home composting.

Home composting comes with several restrictions. Biodegradable plastics are out, as mentioned earlier, but there is more to consider. It takes effort to get the right mix of green and brown matter and control the water content. Backyard compost bins aren't the best place for animal products, such as skin and bones from meat and fish, because these items are likely to attract live animals. Even if the bin is covered, it probably wouldn't be safe from raccoons. Also, the smell from rotting meat might not be something you want in your backyard.

It's probably best to stick to fruit and vegetable scraps along with grass clippings and leaves.

COMPOSTING BIODEGRADABLE PLASTICS

Biodegradable servingware and food containers are designed to be industrially compostable, meaning that they degrade under the specific conditions of composition, temperature, and humidity present at an industrial composting facility. To be industrially compostable, biodegradable plastics must:

- Degrade at least 90% by weight within six months at an industrial composting facility
- Contain at least 50% organic matter
- Contain no more than a specified concentration of heavy metals
- Disintegrate into fragments smaller than 2 mm within twelve weeks under controlled composting conditions
- Create compost that is nontoxic, meaning that it will create no negative health effects when used as a soil amendment for food crops

Biodegradable plastics are those items that look like plastic and can be difficult to distinguish from conventional plastic cups or forks. If you look closely, a compostable plastic cup will probably be labeled with what looks like a recycling symbol and the number 7, for "other." As explained on page 56, the symbol does not mean that the cup can be recycled. Biodegradable plastics should not go in the recycling bin.

We shouldn't have to inspect products with a magnifying glass or decode markings to determine whether they belong in a compost bin or a trash can (standard plastic cutlery is not recyclable either). For this reason, clear labeling should be a priority. Progress is being made. I've seen containers at natural food stores bearing the words "compostable in industrial facilities" and "do not recycle" in large letters. But such labeling is far from universal.

Biodegradable plastics do not belong in a backyard compost bin because they will not degrade fast enough, due to typically lower composting temperature and the lack of grinders to chop them into small pieces. Even in an industrial facility, such items do not add to the value of the resulting compost. They do, at least, degrade sufficiently to not be detrimental, although some people would argue with that assertion. Not all facilities accept compostable plastic cups and cutlery. The city of Portland, Oregon, for example, only accepts food waste and uncoated paper into compost.

Compostable clamshell packaging, designed to replace Styrofoam or clear plastic clamshells, is a different story. The clamshells look like cardboard and are made from fiberboard sourced from agricultural waste. Sources include wheat straw—the stalks that are left behind after removing the edible part of the wheat plant—and leftover sugar cane stalks. All composting programs that accept food waste should also accept fiberboard containers.

KEY TAKEAWAYS

➤ Organic waste will not degrade rapidly in a landfill and will release methane when it does degrade.

➤ Options for composting food waste include curbside collection for transport to an industrial composting facility, community composting programs, and backyard or patio compost bins. Most communities lack access to curbside collection.

➤ Industrial composting facilities grind up organic waste and process it in controlled conditions of temperature and humidity so it will degrade within weeks or months.

➤ Biodegradable plastics will only degrade properly in an industrial composting facility and should not be put into a backyard compost bin. They are not recyclable.

➤ Uncoated fiberboard containers and plain cardboard and paper can be composted with food waste and yard trimmings.

CHAPTER 4

WASTE STREAMS

The first step in taking control of the waste you generate is to examine it. Have you considered all the different types of items and materials you discard? Once you stop and look at everything you toss out, you may be surprised by both the quantity and the variety.

In Chapter 1, you learned that Americans discard an average of 4.5 to 8 pounds of waste per person per day. That's between 135 and 240 pounds per month per person, or between 540 and 960 pounds for a household of four. How you do think you compare to the average American? Do you generate your weight in waste every month? I encourage you to make a guess now. Write it down or mark a box below, and then return to that guess when you get to Chapter 5. That chapter will teach you how to measure your waste for a month and see how close you come to your estimate.

I believe that my household generates this much waste per person per day:

	Less than 1 pound
	2-4 pounds
	4-6 pounds
	6-8 pounds
	8-10 pounds
	More than 10 pounds

This chapter includes sections describing many common types of waste and options available for handling it. The sections explain why certain items are or are not recyclable or compostable. Each section includes a checklist where you can note which types of waste you generate and mark whether it belongs in the trash (landfill), recycling, or composting bin.

The bins are not the only possible destination for your waste. In some cases, other disposal options exist, such as taking items to a drop-off location for reuse or recycling. Some cities run special recycling events that accept many types of hard-to-recycle items. Taking advantage of these events requires saving up items instead of tossing them into the garbage bin.

Your options depend on the available services in your area. You may or may not have an industrial composting facility in your city or county. You may have a single recycling bin that accepts paper, plastic, glass, and metal, or you may be expected to presort your recyclables (see page 25 in Chapter 2 for more information about waste sorting). Certain items that are considered recyclable in one city are not allowed in another. If you live in an apartment building, your options may be different than if you live in a single-family home.

Before filling out the checklists in this chapter, you will need to know how your area processes waste. For example, residents of Seattle can find comprehensive information at https://www.seattle.gov/utilities/services/where-does-it-go#/categories explaining what belongs in the garbage, recycling, and yard waste bins. If you live elsewhere in the US, I recommend looking up the website of your city government or local waste collection company, where there should be resources describing how to handle the various types of materials listed in this chapter. If you aren't sure which company collects your waste, an Internet search for your city or county plus "recycling" or "waste" should turn up the result you need.

If the advice on the website for your community contradicts what this book says, go with the website. As mentioned earlier, the guidelines are not universal. The examples in this chapter often pertain to a specific city or region and are correct as of the time of publication.

Food waste

An estimated 50 million tons of compostable materials, mostly made up of food waste, headed to landfills in 2015.[1] That's an average of 5 pounds per person every week. Throwing away less food ranks third in Project Drawdown's list of important ways to reduce global carbon emissions.[2] Most household food waste is completely avoidable.

Leftover or spoiled food is often thrown away because that is the most convenient option. Composting, if available, is a much better choice. Composting is especially convenient for people like me who live in a city that accepts food waste in the curbside yard waste bin. My city even provides me a free three-gallon container to collect the compost. I keep the small container under the sink, line it with a compostable bag, and drop the full bag into my curbside bin a few times a week. Unlike when I lived in an area without this service, I rarely use the disposal in the kitchen sink.

I recognize that most people in the US don't have access to industrial composting that accepts food waste. As recently as 2017, fewer than 2% of communities in the US could deposit food waste into a curbside bin.[3] Your local waste management company's website should inform you about whether curbside composting is available in your area. If not, you may have access to a drop-off facility. A backyard compost bin (see Chapter 3) is another option.

Smarter shopping strategies, including not overbuying just because something is on sale, and diligent use of leftovers, make it easy to minimize food waste. You can save money while also conserving resources (water, energy, packaging) that would be used to produce food that ends up as trash. This is especially important if you don't have an at-home compost option, but it's a good idea even if you do compost.

Scraps, Peels, and Stems: Recipes and Tips for Rethinking Food Waste at Home by Jill Lightner includes many creative ways to use scraps that would otherwise become waste. She mentions making stock from chicken bones and saving up onion and carrot trimmings in the freezer to use in vegetable or meat stock. I was already doing this before I read Lightner's book, but to many readers, it may be a completely new idea.

Not everything can be reused, but a surprising variety of food scraps can find a second life before being dumped into the trash or compost. The worksheet on page 71 is a handy place to gather ideas for reducing food waste at home. A fillable PDF version is available at https://juliagoldsteinauthor.com/worksheets.

One more piece of advice: for the most part, disregard "best by" or "use by" dates on packaged food. These dates do not mean that the food is spoiled after the date printed on the package or that it will make you sick if you eat it. It is merely a suggestion from the manufacturer as to how long the food will be freshest or most flavorful.

Common sense is the best approach. If you're not sure if the food is still edible, smell it and look at it. If it smells and looks fine, taste it. If it tastes fine, it's good to eat even if the date on it has passed. If it is moldy or foul-smelling, toss it regardless of the date on the package. You can also find guidelines on best practices for food safety on the US Department of Agriculture website, usda.gov.

Yard trimmings

Yard trimmings are not a primary worry when it comes to recycling, but there are still opportunities to switch to best practices that minimize environmental damage. In any case, yard waste does not belong in the trash.

The weight of yard trimmings entering landfills has dropped dramatically since many landfills around the country stopped accepting these materials and many curbside collection programs started including a separate bin for yard waste. These bins take grass clippings, leaves, branches, fallen fruit, and the like. Some communities have regulations on the size of tree branches they will accept. For example, in my community, branches are supposed to be less than 4 inches in diameter. We can dispose of larger branches at the twice-yearly city collection program that takes many types of waste.

A trip to San Jose, California in 2019 reminded me that yard waste in that city doesn't go into a bin. Residents pile it in the street for collection. A truck comes by weekly to scoop it up and take it to a composting facility. For obvious reasons, food scraps can't go with yard trimmings in San Jose.

For those who have lawns to mow, if your lawn mower has a mulching setting, you can just leave the clippings on the grass where they release nutrients back into the soil. Yes, the lawn won't look as pristine as if you collected the clippings in the mower's bag, but it will grow healthier and need less fertilizer.

If your community makes compost from yard trimmings, you should be careful when dealing with diseased plants. Fruit that has been infected with a fungus, for example, isn't going to be healthy for compost that will be used to grow crops.

It's also good to avoid the use of toxic herbicides and pesticides whenever possible. These chemicals wash into local waterways when you water the garden or during the next rain as well as contaminating the yard waste. Less toxic alternatives abound. Growing plants that are native to your area, or at least well-suited to your climate, increases the likelihood that they will thrive with little care. For weeds growing between cracks in the driveway or sidewalk, pouring boiling water on them really works to kill the undesirable plants (I've tried it). Once they are dead, it's easy to pull them up and toss them into the yard waste bin. White vinegar is another option.

PAPER AND PAPER PRODUCTS

Although the days when every household subscribed to a daily newspaper are long gone and the digital age has been with us for decades, household waste still contains a surprisingly large amount of paper. Some is regular mail, from magazines to advertisements.

But much of the paper waste is corrugated cardboard and other paper packaging materials. Online ordering is so easy and, despite recent measures to reduce the amount of packaging required, items often arrive in unnecessarily large packaging, or at the center of so many layers they're reminiscent of Russian nesting dolls. Sometimes different items from one order ship separately because they come from different warehouses, with each shipment needing its own box. Even when we buy items at a store, they often come in multiple cardboard boxes, include paper inserts, or are sealed in plastic films. More on that plastic later.

The good news is that paper is recyclable and more paper is being made from recycled stock. All types of paper that arrive in your mailbox are recyclable, including envelopes with clear plastic windows and glossy advertisements and magazines, assuming you don't contaminate them with food. Paper contaminated with food waste belongs in the yard waste bin (or the trash if you don't have a yard waste bin or composting isn't available). Pizza boxes are an obvious example, but it applies to any greasy food residue that you can't shake off.

It's also important to keep paper waste dry. Wet cardboard and paper will break down, and it's more difficult for MRFs to separate it. For this reason, please don't overfill your bin because if it doesn't close completely, rain will get in. That's more of a concern for those of us in the Pacific Northwest than for residents of Los Angeles or Phoenix, but keeping bins closed is good practice anywhere. Loose paper or plastic can blow away from a partially open bin and drift into storm drains.

Most clean, dry paper products are recyclable, but there are some important exceptions:

▶ Paper mailers filled with bubble wrap

The plastic protects items during shipping but unfortunately makes the packaging nonrecyclable. If you can't easily separate the paper from the plastic, neither can a recycling facility. But although the packaging isn't recyclable, it is reusable. Just put new labels over the old, tape it closed, and avoid a trip to the office supply store before you mail your next package.

▶ Printed store receipts

These may look recyclable, but thermal paper is usually coated with a layer of bisphenol A (BPA) or bisphenol S (BPS). BPA is the same additive that was removed from hard plastic bottles because of the health risks associated with the chemical. BPS is a related chemical that poses similar risks. That coating is not recyclable. Requesting email receipts instead of printed ones is a way to reduce this waste stream, but many stores use systems that print receipts even if the customer doesn't want one. You can also ask the store manager to switch to a bisphenol-free paper the next time they order office supplies.

⟩ Paper cups and plates

Disposable paper coffee cups are not necessarily recyclable because of the polyethylene coating inside them. The coating performs a valuable function—keeping the hot liquid inside the cup from leaking through the paper—but it makes recycling more difficult.

A few paper recycling mills can separate the paper from the plastic and process it, but many mills can't handle coated cups. A better solution? Bring a reusable cup or mug to work and to your local coffee shop.

Paper plates may or may not be compostable depending on whether they are coated with plastic. Compostable paper plates will usually have a matte (not shiny) surface. If you're not sure, it is best to check labels to determine whether paper plates can be safely composted. If you buy compostable ones, you can even take them camping and toss them into the campfire after dinner. You might want to be careful, though, if they have lots of greasy food residue on them that could make the fire burn too hot. Bringing reusable plates sounds like a safer bet.

Unless clearly marked as compostable, plastic-lined paper plates and cups do not belong with compost. As of early 2020, Starbucks was evaluating a new type of paper cup that is both recyclable and compostable. I find this announcement especially intriguing because in my book, *Material Value,* I imagined an "ideal plastic" that would possess all the benefits of existing plastics and none of the drawbacks. This ideal material would be recyclable, nontoxic, and biodegradable.

Aseptic containers

These are the rectangular boxes used to package soups, broth, juices, and other liquid food products. They contain multiple layers, including paper and plastic. But these containers can sometimes be accepted for recycling. For more details, see the multilayer packaging section on page 66.

Paper towels and napkins

These items are compostable in locations where curbside bins accept food waste. If composting is not an option, they must be thrown in the trash if they are contaminated with food. The cardboard tubes from paper towels and toilet paper are recyclable.

♻

The chart on page 72 lists common paper products you are likely to encounter along with a place to mark how to handle each one. A fillable PDF version is available at https://juliagoldsteinauthor.com/worksheets.

METALS

Metal waste from households is mostly containers from canned goods. These containers are recyclable, but they should be washed clean of food and shaken dry. It probably is not necessary to remove paper labels unless your city specifies otherwise.

Rules about how to handle metal lids vary. Some cities advise crimping metal cans with the lid inside and others can process loose lids. Some recycling policies specify a minimum diameter for lids, which means that metal lids on glass jars are more likely recyclable than bottle caps on glass beverage containers. But you could crimp a bunch of bottle caps inside a metal can. You can use a household magnet to distinguish between steel and aluminum bottle caps. Steel will be drawn to the magnet, while aluminum will not. Separating aluminum and steel helps streamline recycling at processing plants, where each type of metal gets recycled individually.

Aluminum foil may or may not be recyclable. In Seattle, for example, clean aluminum foil or food pans can go in recycling, but the city says not to crumple the foil into a ball. Metal that is contaminated with food must be discarded in the trash. Regardless of your city's policies, you can often reuse foil several times before it becomes torn or too contaminated with food to reuse.

Wire coat hangers are usually not accepted in the recycling bin, but dry cleaners will generally take them for reuse. You can drop off hangers even if you don't have clothes in need of dry cleaning.

Scrap metal left over from broken objects or home repairs may be acceptable in your recycling bin, but it can also find other destinations. Scrap yards will often buy it, the price per pound varying depending on the type of metal. Discarded copper pipes are worth more than pieces of steel. The iScrap App (available for iPhone and Android) shows locations of scrap yards and lists current prices.

All sorts of metal objects—nuts and screws, coat hangers, broken garden tools—may be of interest to artists. The market for art made from recycled materials is exploding. If you're interested in pursuing this, the book *Start a Creative Recycling Side Hustle: 101 Ideas for Making Money from Sustainable Crafts Consumers Crave* by James

Dillehay is full of practical advice for artists and aspiring artists wanting to jump on board.

You can use the worksheet on page 73 to list the types of metal you may have at your house and decide what to do with it. A fillable PDF version is available at https://juliagoldsteinauthor.com/worksheets.

PLASTICS

Plastic is one of the most troubling categories of household waste. As discussed in Chapter 2, plastic comes in so many forms, only some of which are recyclable at the curbside. Containers that were accepted prior to 2018 may no longer be accepted because of changes stemming from the new rules about sending recyclables overseas. When in doubt, look it up.

Many types of plastic packaging can be reused at home to store food or other items. But if it's damaged or you decide you don't want to keep it, it's important to dispose of it properly.

The numbers on plastic containers indicate the type of plastic but not whether the item is recyclable. Even though that triangle looks like a recycling symbol, don't be fooled.

Numbers 1 through 6 are for specific plastics. Most curbside recyclers take containers labeled #1 (polyethylene terephthalate, PET), #2 (high-density polyethylene, HDPE), and sometimes #5 (polypropylene). Some cities and counties group products by shape instead of number because that approach allows them to sort the recyclables more efficiently and improve the real recycling rate. Curbside recycling where I live, for example, only wants bottles, jugs, cups, and tubs. Lids are accepted only if firmly attached to containers.

Number	Material	Examples	Accepted Curbside?
♲1	Polyethylene terephthalate, PET	Water bottles, some clam-shells	Depends on shape
♲2	High-density polyethylene, HDPE	Milk jugs	Depends on shape
♲3	Polyvinyl chloride, PVC	Plumbing	No
♲4	Low-density poly-ethylene, LDPE.	Grocery bags, reclosable baggies	No
♲5	Polypropylene	Yogurt tubs	Depends on shape
♲6	Polystyrene	Styrofoam cups	No
♲7	Other	Nylon, compostable plastics	No

Plastic grocery bags, bread bags, zip-top baggies, and other similar lightweight packaging is made from plastic #4, low-density polyethylene (LDPE). These products should be kept out of general plastic recycling streams, unless your city accepts large plastic bags filled with smaller bags, but they can be recycled.

Many communities place bins in grocery stores specifically to collect #4 plastic, which gets "downcycled" into plastic lumber and similar products where the exact composition of the recycled material isn't critical. These bins typically accept a wide range of lightweight plastics including plastic wrap (Saran Wrap® and similar products) and bubble wrap.

The V in the logo for type #3 stands for vinyl, as in polyvinyl chloride (PVC). Such materials are not recyclable. PVC tubing might be accepted at locations that collect construction debris for salvage.

Polystyrene (Styrofoam), type #6, isn't usually accepted in curbside recycling. Mixing it in will contaminate the recycling stream and may cause an entire load to be sent to a landfill. Some communities collect type #6 plastic separately if they have a local facility that will recycle Styrofoam packaging. If recycling is available for Styrofoam food containers, those need to be washed to remove any food residue.

Type #7, "other," is any plastic other than types 1 through 6. This includes polycarbonate, the hard plastics that reusable water bottles are made from, as well as compostable plastics. Nylon also falls under the category of "other." Even though the material is recyclable, it doesn't belong in curbside recycling. Industrial nylon production collects scraps for melting and processing. Nylon and polyester fabrics, of course, fall into the category of textiles (see page 68).

Compostable cups and flatware should not go into the blue bin. They are most likely made from polylactic acid (PLA), which is designed to degrade in an industrial composting facility (see Chapter 3 for more about industrial composting). If you live in a neighborhood where curbside collection allows compostable plastics, you can put them in with food waste. If not, they must go to landfill. Do not put them with mixed plastic recycling where they will contaminate the recycling stream.

The guidelines in this section are helpful but not comprehensive. I suggest that you keep your city or county recycling guide handy when filling out the form on page 74. It's a convenient place to list all the plastics you are likely to encounter. A fillable PDF version is available at https://juliagoldsteinauthor.com/worksheets.

A note on bagging groceries. Plastic grocery bags are not necessarily worse for the environment than paper bags, so long as they are disposed of properly and not allowed to escape into local waterways. Producing a paper bag requires four times as much water as producing a plastic bag and creates three times the carbon emissions. Paper bags must be made from virgin rather than recycled paper to be strong enough to hold groceries. But paper bags hold more than plastic bags and they are compostable and recyclable. Reusable bags are the best option if they are reused as intended. The environmental impact of making a cotton bag is more than 100 times that of making a plastic bag, so if you invest in one, be prepared to use it regularly.[4]

GLASS

Glass can be recycled multiple times through a process that creates high-quality recycled glass. Various types of glass, however, have different compositions and melting points. Some glass, such as that in vintage glassware or old windows, contains heavy metals like lead that should be kept out of the recycling stream. Most bottles and jars from foods and beverages, regardless of color, are recyclable.

Just because glass bottles are recyclable, however, doesn't mean they are accepted in all curbside recycling programs. Glass recycling rates average 33% in the US compared to 90% in Europe. There are two reasons: transportation distance and contamination rates.

Some US states don't allow curbside glass recycling because there are no local processing facilities and the cost of shipping the heavy glass hundreds of miles or more is too high to justify. The only glass processing plants in the northwestern US, for example, are in Seattle, Washington, and Portland, Oregon. There are no plants between Seattle and Minneapolis.

Contamination poses another barrier to glass recycling. Food residue is not the only problem. When people discard small pieces of plastic and metal into their recycling bins, those go through screens at the MRF and end up in a pile with the broken glass.

The increased prevalence of single-stream recycling in the US has resulted in a dirtier stream of glass. Clean glass, like that received from regions where glass is collected separately, is worth much more per ton. The economics of recycling mean that highly contaminated glass isn't valuable enough for it to get recycled. MRFs aren't paid much for glass contaminated with nonrecyclable glass, metal, plastic, and garbage, so they can't sell it without losing money. It costs more to separate and ship than the glass is worth.

The Closed Loop Foundation completed a study in 2017 examining ways to increase recycling of glass at MRFs. The study targeted facilities located within 100 miles of a glass processing plant. They reported declining rates of glass recycling and suggested that if MRFs invested in better cleaning systems, they could produce a more valuable stream of ground glass free from contaminants. They could presumably resell it at a rate that justifies the up-front expense of the equipment.[5]

If you live in California, Connecticut, Hawaii, Iowa, Maine, Massachusetts, Michigan, New York, Oregon, or Vermont, you can drop off glass bottles and receive money back. These ten states have enacted container deposit laws, also known at bottle bills. Retail stores pay distributors five or ten cents per bottle purchased, the cost is included in the purchase price, and consumers get a rebate when they return empty bottles to a store or redemption center. Details about which types of beverage bottles qualify vary from state to state, but plastic or metal bottles can also be eligible for rebates.

These programs work. In Michigan, where the deposit is ten cents compared to five cents for most other states with bottle bills, the recycling rate for eligible containers is 92%, higher than that of states with five-cent deposits and much higher than for states without bottle bills.[6] Glass bottle recycling rates in all states with bottle bills is around 90%, similar to that in Europe and far above the 33% average for the US.

Until container deposit laws spread across the country, residents of most states have fewer options. They can place glass containers in their recycling bins if curbside recycling is available. If not, glass bottles and jars might have to go into the landfill. If your MRF is going to send it to a landfill anyway, there's not much point in putting glass into a curbside recycling bin unless doing so will allow the glass to be used as landfill cover. You can ask your local waste hauler what happens to glass if you put it into the trash bin or with the recycling.

As with metal, however, glass is a great material for recycled art. A vendor at my local outdoor market sells decorative scented candles that come in recycled glass bottles.

The worksheet on page 75 provides a place to list disposal options for common types of glass. A fillable PDF version is available at https://juliagoldsteinauthor.com/worksheets.

E-WASTE

Those of us who live in states where e-waste collection has been the norm for a decade or more are accustomed to turning in old cell phones, computers, and other electronics at dedicated collection spots. But only half the states in the US have e-waste regulations (see map).[7] In the rest of the country, people are either stashing obsolete electronic devices in their homes or throwing them out with their garbage. Even in the states with e-waste programs, old electronics often gather dust rather than being recycled. E-waste collection rates are a dismal 20%.[8]

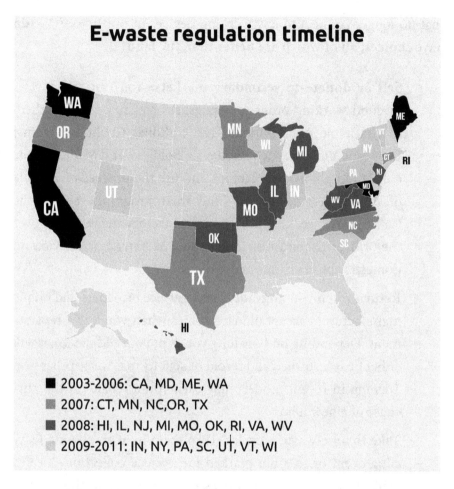

E-waste regulation timeline

- 2003-2006: CA, MD, ME, WA
- 2007: CT, MN, NC,OR, TX
- 2008: HI, IL, NJ, MI, MO, OK, RI, VA, WV
- 2009-2011: IN, NY, PA, SC, UT, VT, WI

Electronic devices are designed with frequent replacement in mind. We can, of course, choose how frequently to replace our devices. I try to extend the lifespan of the electronics in my house as long as possible, but I'm dismayed by how many laptops I've gone through in the past five years. They keep malfunctioning despite my desperate attempts to get them repaired.

What are the options once our devices no longer work or we want to upgrade them? What can we do with the stash of cords and cables that no longer connect to any working devices in our house? **We do have choices, all of which are better than the landfill.**

> ➤ **Sell or donate to secondary markets.** You can sell devices in good working order on Craigslist or eBay or donate them to charitable organizations. The National Coalition Against Domestic Violence, Cell Phones for Soldiers, and Medic Mobile collect old phones and laptops and use the proceeds from sale of refurbished devices to fund their programs. Secure the Call restores working cell phones to factory defaults, removes the SIM cards, and distributes them as emergency devices to domestic abuse victims and seniors.

> ➤ **Return when you upgrade.** Many service providers and phone manufacturers accept old electronics when you buy a replacement. Depending on how long you kept your old device, it will either be refurbished and resold or sent to an e-waste processor. Turning in recent models may earn you a rebate on the purchase of a new item.

> ➤ **Take to an e-waste recycler.** Turn them in at an e-waste recycling event or to a bin marked for e-waste collection. Ideally, your electronics will be processed somewhere in the US and the materials inside the devices will be recycled to make new products. In the Seattle area, Ridwell (see page 34) accepts electronics as one of its rotating categories and sends devices for local processing.

Unfortunately, responsible e-waste processing can be difficult to verify. I gave a talk in 2019 at the University of Washington (UW) where I discussed the story of Total Reclaim, an e-waste processor that had been fined millions of dollars for illegally sending e-waste overseas instead of processing it domestically. The company's actions violated regulations from the Washington State Department of Ecology. The states of Washington and Oregon successfully sued Total Reclaim.

During the question and answer period after my UW presentation, a student mentioned that there were bins on campus for depositing old cell phones. Another student pulled out her phone and did a search to determine where the e-waste went. She showed me her screen. In 2012, UW was using Total Reclaim! She couldn't find any more recent information.

Before dropping off e-waste, it's best to dig a bit to find out which company is going to process it. Companies that are certified to the R2 standard commit to following best practices for environmental health and safety. There are no guarantees, but increased awareness is improving e-waste processing. If everything you find on the company's website makes a convincing argument that the e-waste will be sent to a secondary market or responsibly recycled, the recycler is probably a good choice. It's also helpful to check whether the recycler will wipe data from your devices or whether you should do that in advance as a precaution.

Some e-waste recyclers consider nearly anything that uses electricity to be e-waste. You can drop off a nonfunctioning coffee maker or toaster, or that random box of cords and cables with plugs that are not compatible with anything in your house. Other facilities are more particular and only take items like phones, tablets, and laptops. Dropping off large electronics such as TVs may require paying a fee. You will need to remove the batteries from any electronic device and recycle those separately.

You can list your available e-waste recycling options in the form on page 76.

Hazardous waste

Hazardous waste is usually associated with industries such as mining, oil and gas, and chemicals. But households generate hazardous waste as well. Homeowners who do their own gardening or repairs use hazardous products, but many common items that many people assume are harmless fall into the category of hazardous waste. These include:

> Oil-based paints and stains

> Glues and adhesives

> Motor oil

> Fluorescent light bulbs

> Nail polish

If you're not sure whether your household waste is hazardous, look it up on your city or county waste disposal website. Tossing hazardous waste into the garbage causes it to contaminate landfills with toxins that get into the soil and water. King County, where I live, maintains a list of more than 80 categories of items with instructions on how to handle them. In general, if a product is labeled "CAUTION," "WARNING," "DANGER," or "POISON," it probably needs to go to a designated hazardous waste disposal site. In addition, some products that are not toxic are classified as hazardous waste because they are flammable and therefore pose a danger if tossed into a landfill.

While oil-based paint qualifies as hazardous waste, water-based paint generally does not. Mixing old latex paint with cat litter does work to solidify it, but once you do so, you are choosing to send it to a landfill. You can instead take unwanted paint to a location that collects it for recycling. These places charge a small fee per gallon to take usable open containers of paint, filter them, and blend them to make new paint in a range of colors. The fee covers the extra cost of processing the used paint.

A note on light bulbs: With LED light bulbs becoming more common, lighting is now part of the e-waste stream. Fortunately, LED bulbs last many years, unless you buy a dud. Occasionally they stop working within months of being installed and must be discarded as e-waste. At least they no longer cost so much that a faulty LED bulb seems like such a waste of money.

When replacing older light bulbs with LEDs, incandescent bulbs—the ones with the tungsten filaments—can go in the trash. But fluorescent bulbs must be treated as hazardous waste and disposed of at a location that's willing to take them. Home improvement stores or drugstores in your area may have collection bins designated for fluorescent bulbs.

The form on page 77 lists many common types of hazardous household waste. You can look up how to handle each one by searching online for "hazardous waste" and your city or county. E-waste is not listed because it is discussed separately in the previous section. See https://juliagoldsteinauthor.com/worksheets for a fillable PDF version of the form.

After reviewing the form and examining the contents of your cabinets, you may ask yourself whether you even want some of these materials in your home. If you want to reduce the need to dispose of hazardous waste in the first place, safer options exist for many of the products listed on the form. The book *101 Ways to Go Zero Waste* includes recipes for homemade, nontoxic alternatives to common household cleaning and gardening products. In many cases these work just as well as the commercial products, while with others you may need to use the products more frequently or add extra elbow grease.

MIXED MATERIALS

Packaging doesn't always fall neatly into a single category such as paper, plastic, or metal. Whether for protecting food or shipping fragile products, multilayer packaging is commonplace. Determining whether such packaging is recyclable is not easy. Here are some general guidelines for several popular types of composite, or multilayer, packaging.

Aseptic containers

These are the rectangular boxes used to package soups, broth, juices, and other liquid food products. They typically consist of six layers. The primary structural material is paperboard, a thick paper. The paperboard is coated on both sides with a plastic film, usually polyethylene, to protect the paper from moisture. An interior layer of aluminum keeps out oxygen and unwanted odors and extends the shelf life of the food or drink inside the package. The food contact layer is polyethylene.

Aseptic containers are often recyclable even though the various layers can't be easily separated. Because of the difficulty in separating the layers, the packages are shredded and made into lower value products such as roof shingles or plastic lumber. Not all cities accept these containers in recycling bins, so it's best to check before tossing them in.

Multilayer pouches

This is the type of packaging used for Capri Sun brand juices, prepared tuna salad, and similar foodstuffs. The plastic packaging team of the American Chemistry Council makes bold claims about plastic pouch sustainability. Proponents who have a vested economic interest talk about the benefits of these pouches. They protect food and prolong its shelf life without adding preservatives that consumers don't want to see in their food, thus reducing food waste. Plastic pouches are efficient. Overall packaging weight and dimensions are smaller than for the same food packaged in cardboard boxes with plastic liners, so transportation costs and associated environmental impacts are lower.

But how about packaging waste? These pouches, which are often made from multiple plastics and sometimes include layers of foil or paper, are typically not recyclable. To avoid contaminating the recycling stream, only place multilayer pouches in a recycling bin if your city accepts them. And be sure to rinse them out.

Padded mailers

Envelopes for shipping fragile items often incorporate a layer of padding for protection. Sometimes the padding resembles plastic bubble wrap. This type of envelope, unfortunately, is usually not recyclable. It seems strange, since the composition of paper plus polyethylene resembles aseptic containers. But the logistics of sorting plastic-filled paper mailers and separating them from those without plastic must not be worth the trouble.

It's important to examine mailing envelopes carefully. Those padded with paper can go into general or paper recycling. Envelopes made from only plastic can be recycled in the grocery store bins dedicated to lightweight plastic bags and films (see page 56). Sometimes the labeling on envelopes can help identify how to handle them.

Mailing envelopes are, however, reusable if you remove the address label or attach a new one that covers the previous label. I save padded envelopes to mail out signed copies of my books and include a note with information about how to reuse or recycle the envelope.

The worksheet on page 78 lists common multilayer products you are likely to encounter along with a place to mark how to handle each one. A fillable PDF version is available at https://juliagoldsteinauthor.com/worksheets.

TEXTILES

What do you do with used clothing? If it's in good condition, you can donate it to a thrift store or charitable organization that accepts clothing donations. Some communities have collection bins that take shoes and clothing. You can sell high-end, gently worn clothing to consignment stores. If you instead prefer to keep your clothing as long as possible, consignment stores can be great places to look for bargains on used clothing in excellent condition.

Many people toss outdated or damaged clothing into the garbage bin, but this is a mistake. In many regions, charities like Goodwill now accept clothing in any condition. You can even toss in stained or torn clothing, mismatched socks, old underwear, and bedding. If clothing is not in good enough condition to sell, it gets recycled. Recycled textiles can become cleaning rags or get processed into fibers for insulation, padding, or various industrial uses.

If you have a full bag of unsaleable textiles, it helps to mark it as such when donating, to save the employees from having to sort through it. And only bring damaged textiles to places that say that they accept these items and will recycle them.

You can, of course, use worn-out textiles as cleaning rags at home or find other uses for them. When the bottom sheet of a set became too torn to use, I took the top sheet and made it into two dozen cloth napkins. I know people who take old t-shirts that have sentimental value and sew them into a quilt. Fabric scraps are another of those categories of materials that are great for making into recycled art.

Availability of textile recycling varies depending on where you live. In the Seattle area, Threadcycle (http://www.kingcounty.gov/threadcycle) maintains drop boxes where residents can deposit used textiles, and Ridwell (http://www.ridwell.com) collects textiles bi-weekly.

Simple Recycling (https://simplerecycling.com) operates in many cities around the US including Chicago, Minneapolis, and Dallas, and keeps adding more locations. The company provides bags for residents to fill and drop off with their curbside trash and recycling. Items in good condition can be resold in local thrift stores. The next tier heads to secondhand markets overseas, and the rest will get recycled.

The primary takeaway? Don't throw away old clothing, shoes, or bedding unless it is mildewed or contaminated with hazardous waste. Make sure everything is clean and dry (to avoid causing mildew) and find a collection facility in your neighborhood. You can even donate pillows and stuffed animals if you find a place that will take them.

The chart on page 79 includes a list of items that you can probably sell, donate, or send for recycling. A fillable PDF version is available at https://juliagoldsteinauthor.com/worksheets.

THE WORKSHEETS

The pages at the end of this chapter include worksheets that allow you to create personalized lists of which items are recyclable where you live. Feel free to indicate first and second choices for disposal if you have more than one option and add items beyond those already listed for each category of waste.

The information in this chapter, the website of your local recycling or waste hauling company, and the list of websites in the Resources section (page 106) are all helpful sources of information. Downloadable PDFs of the worksheets are available at https://juliagoldsteinauthor.com/worksheets.

Key takeaways

➤ Reducing waste involves more than just dealing with plastics; this chapter discusses ten categories of household waste.

➤ Options for handling waste may include taking items to a drop-off location for reuse or recycling.

➤ Available disposal methods vary by location and type of material.

➤ When in doubt, check with your local waste hauling company or look up recycling services for your city.

Ideas for Reducing Food Waste

Type of waste	Plan of action	Date started

Note: you can create SMART goals around these (see worksheet on page 96)

Destinations for Paper and Paperboard Waste

Item description	Recycling bin	Yard waste/ compost bin	Landfill	Notes
Advertising inserts (glossy)				
Bills and other mail				
Coffee cups, lined				
Corrugated cardboard boxes				
Magazines and catalogs				
Mailing envelopes, bubble padded				
Mailing envelopes, paper only				
Napkins and paper towels				
Newspaper				
Paper egg cartons				
Paper plates				
Paper towel and toilet paper tubes				
Pizza boxes				
Store receipts (thermal paper)				

Notes: how to prepare for recycling, alternate deposit location, etc.

Destinations for Metal Waste

Item description	Recycling bin	Take to scrap yard	Landfill	Notes
Coat hangers				
Food cans				
Hardware (screws, bolts, etc.)				
Lids from jars (large)				
Lids from jars (small)				
Scrap aluminum				
Scrap copper				
Scrap metal (other)				
Scrap steel				

Notes: how to prepare for recycling, size requirements for lids, etc.

Name and location of scrap yards

_____

_____

Destinations for Plastic Waste

Item description	Recycling bin	Grocery store drop-off	Landfill	Notes
Bubble wrap				
Clear plastic bowls				
Clear plastic clamshells				
Cutlery (forks, spoons, knives)				
Film (cling wrap)				
Jars with metal lids				
Jars with plastic lids				
Milk jugs				
Plastic grocery bags				
Reclosable baggies				
Styrofoam food containers				
Styrofoam packaging (non-food)				
Water and soft drink bottles				
Yogurt/cheese/dairy tubs				

Notes: Preferred options, whether lids should be on or off, how to prepare for recycling, alternate deposit option, etc.

Destinations for Glass Waste

Item description	Curbside recycling bin	Return for deposit	Landfill	Notes
Beer bottles				
Broken glass				
Food containers				
Incandescent light bulbs				
Mirrors				
Soda bottles				
Vases				
Windows				
Wine bottles				

Notes: how to prepare for recycling, alternate deposit location, etc.

Destinations for Electronic Waste (e-waste)

Drop-off locations: _____

_____

_____

Resale options: _____

_____

_____

Item description	Resell	Donate	Curbside pickup	Notes
Cell phones				
Cords and cables				
Desktop computers				
LED light bulbs				
Monitors				
Remote controls				
Small electronics				
Small kitchen appliances				
Tablets/laptops/ e-readers				
TVs				

Note: some e-waste collection facilities only accept specific types of e-waste, and some charge fees for large items like TVs. Batteries will need to be removed.

Handling of Hazardous Waste

Item category	Hazardous waste disposal	Alternative disposal option	Notes
Aerosol cans, pressurized			
All-purpose cleaners			
Antibacterial products and disinfectants			
Antifreeze			
Automotive fluids and oils			
Batteries, automotive			
Batteries, household			
Brake fluid			
Bug/insect killer			
Butane and propane tanks			
Charcoal			
Chlorine bleach			
Drain opener/cleaner			
Epoxy/glue			
Fertilizer			
Fire extinguishers			
Fluorescent light bulbs			
Fungicides			
Gasoline/fuel			
Hair color			
Lawn and garden pesticides			
Lead-based paints			
Lice shampoo			
Motor oil			
Nail polish & remover			
Oil filters			
Oil-based paints and stains			
Oven cleaner			
Paint thinner			
Pepper spray			
Spot and stain remover			
Spray paint			
Thermometers with mercury			
Toilet bowl cleaner			
Weed killers			

Notes: locations for proper disposal, nonhazardous alternatives, etc.

URL for hazardous waste handling information: _____

Destinations for Multilayer and Miscellaneous Waste

Item description	Curbside recycling bin	Take to drop-off location	Landfill	Notes
Boxes from soup, juice, etc.				
Latex paint				
Multilayer pouches				
Padded mailing envelopes				
Toothpaste tubes				

Notes: how to prepare for recycling, alternate deposit location, etc.

Destinations for Textile Waste

Drop-off locations: _____
_____
_____

Resale options: _____
_____
_____

Item description	Resell	Donate	Curb-side pickup	Notes
Backpacks and purses				
Belts				
Clothing, designer/new				
Clothing, lower quality				
Curtains and draperies				
Hats				
Pillows				
Sheets				
Shoes				
Sleeping bags				
Stuffed animals				
Torn and stained clothing				
Towels				

Before dropping off textiles for resale or recycling, please check what items the organization accepts, in what condition, and what type of presorting you need to do.

CHAPTER 5

TRACK YOUR WASTE

Now that you understand more about the processing of garbage and recyclables and have learned how your city or county handles these items, it is time for action. I present several options, ranging from simple to more involved.

For those who love data, I suggest a two-step process: (1) measure your waste and (2) control it by reducing what comes in and properly disposing of what is going out. You can repeat the steps in a loop for continuous improvement. The following sections describe the options for tracking waste generation.

If tracking your waste in detail feels like too much trouble, you might want to skip directly to the section on SMART goals that begins on page 84.

MEASURE IT

If you want to reduce the amount of waste you generate, it is helpful to have a baseline to measure against. Unlike electricity, natural gas, or water use, where utility companies provide their customers a monthly or bi-monthly report, there's no easy way to look up your household monthly waste generation. Even the companies that collect trash and recycling don't have accurate data on how much of what types of waste they are collecting. You can, however, track household waste yourself.

Here are three methods:

- ➤ Track by volume (simpler but not as accurate)
- ➤ Track by weight (more trouble but more accurate)
- ➤ Track by counting (works best for packaging waste)

Tracking by volume is straightforward so long as you know the capacity of your curbside bins. Simply note how long it takes you to fill each bin to track how much material you are sending to landfill, recycling, and compost or yard waste. If your waste hauler provides a calendar of regular and holiday pickup dates, that can be a convenient place to check off when you fill the bin.

Volume tracking can have a financial benefit if you live in an area where your monthly garbage and recycling bill is based on the size of your trash bin. If you find that it always takes longer than a week to fill the bin, you can switch to a smaller size. Doing so will save money on your garbage bill and might encourage your neighbors to wonder why your garbage bin is smaller than theirs. Maybe they will even ask. The next step once you reduce your bin size is to challenge yourself to keep the amount of landfill-bound waste you generate to a level that won't overflow the smaller bin.

For regions with single-stream curbside recycling, which has become the norm in the US, the volume tracking method won't tell you the composition of your recycling stream, unless you fill separate containers inside your house and track their volume before dumping them into the large mixed recycling bin.

The form on page 93 allows you to track your waste by volume. It includes options for mixing all the recyclables and for separating them into two or more streams. A fillable PDF version is available at https://juliagoldsteinauthor.com/worksheets.

❁

Tracking by weight is especially instructive if you want to know how much paper, plastic, and glass you are sending for recycling. National data on trash and recycling tracks the number of tons generated, so you can compare your results to national averages.

Weight tracking emphasizes how much glass weighs, highlighting the problem of transporting heavy loads of glass over long distances.

If you made an estimate in Chapter 4 (page 45), now is the time to test the accuracy of your guess. The form on page 93 allows you to track your waste by weight. It divides recyclables into paper, plastic, glass, and metal. The form doesn't include other categories of items from Chapter 4 since those aren't usually accepted in curbside recycling or aren't something that a typical household discards every week. A fillable PDF version of the form is available at https://juliagoldsteinauthor.com/worksheets.

❁

Tracking by counting, the third method, takes more diligence than volume tracking but is simpler than tracking by weight. You simply count various items before putting them into the recycling bin or the trash. This method has the advantage of informing you about what types of disposable packaging you are using or how much food you are wasting each month. Your results may surprise you and encourage you to switch brands of some products, buy smaller quantities of perishables, or stop buying some products entirely.

If you wish to track your waste using the counting method, you can use the form on page 94. That version has some popular items already listed. If you prefer to create a custom list as you accumulate waste, you can use the blank form on the following page. Fillable PDF versions of both forms are available at https://juliagoldsteinauthor.com/worksheets.

Several online tools can help you track waste as well. The Omni Calculator, for example, asks you to input how many plastic items you use per week or per year in various categories. You can combine the worksheet in this book with the online calculator to better understand your annual plastic footprint. This calculator and other similar guides are listed in the Resources section on page 107.

CONTROL IT

Once you know how much waste you generate and understand what types of materials it contains, you are in a better position to manage it and reduce it. If you have gone through the worksheets in Chapter 4, you may have already changed what you toss where.

I hope that you are now only placing items that you know are recyclable curbside into your curbside recycling bins. I hope that you have found locations to properly dispose of waste that is recyclable or reusable but isn't accepted in your curbside bin. I hope that you are only placing compostable waste in your yard waste bin (if your community provides one).

Placing waste in the correct place is important, but the next step is tackling your waste footprint. I encourage you to write a SMART goal for each action you intend to complete. SMART goals must be:

> Specific: list exactly what you plan to do and put numbers to it,

> Measurable: keep track so you know when you've achieved the goal,

➤ Achievable: choose something that is realistic for you and your family that you can envision doing,

➤ Relevant: know why you're aiming for the goal and choose something that matters to you, and

➤ Time-based: set a concrete deadline.

Here are some suggestions for goals:

➤ Reduce the size of your curbside trash can to the next smaller size available if that is an option where you live.

➤ Fill your recyclables bin once every two or three weeks rather than every week beginning on a specific date. You can set a calendar reminder to keep track of when to set the bin out for city collection.

➤ Buy a food waste container for your kitchen and start composting food waste, either in a curbside bin destined for industrial composting or in a backyard compost bin. Keep a tally of how many times you fill the kitchen container each month.

➤ For one month, each time you receive a piece of physical mail from a business (bills, advertisements, announcements, etc.), set it aside in a designated place or make note of the business that sent it. At the end of the month, contact the businesses and unsubscribe from any mail you no longer wish to receive. If electronic document delivery is an option, you can switch to that for bills and other information you still want.

Feel free to use any of the goals above or create different ones. I suggest revisiting Chapter 4 and creating goals related to each category of waste in that chapter. The book *101 Ways to Go Zero Waste* by Kathryn

Kellogg features a wealth of ideas on ways to reduce waste. You can use the form on page 96 to list your goals and track completion.

♻

I encourage you to share your success stories with me at https://julia-goldsteinauthor.com/contact. If you give me permission, I will share your story with my email subscribers. You are, of course, invited to join my email subscriber list whether or not you have a story to share.

MY EXPERIENCE

I tracked my household waste by weight for a month. It isn't difficult, but honestly, it is a bit tedious. Here's how I conducted the experiment.

➤ Recyclables

I keep a 13-gallon trash can in a hall closet as a temporary holding place for recyclables before they head to the large blue bin outdoors. Before tossing items into the indoor can, I rinsed and dried them as needed and weighed paper, plastic, metal, and glass separately on my kitchen scale. While I don't live in a state with a container deposit law, my curbside recycling program does accept glass.

At the time I ran the experiment, I stored plastic bags separately in a large plastic trash bag hanging in the hall closet. When it got full, I took it to a grocery store drop-off bin. In March 2020, Ridwell (see page 34) started operating in my city and I signed up. Their canvas bag for plastic film has now replaced the plastic trash bag (one fewer bag), and I drop it into the metal box on my front porch for convenient pickup every other week.

As a proponent of reducing waste, perhaps I should be able to boast that I generate no plastic bag waste, but that is not the case. Having a relatively small canvas bag for regular collection, however, makes me more aware of how much plastic film I'm bringing into the house.

One weekend during the month when I initially tracked waste, I painstakingly sorted through stacks of mail that had been accumulating on the kitchen counter. I found overdue bills amongst the junk mail, a sign that I should find a better method for managing the mail. I pay as many bills online as I can, but medical providers in particular insist on sending paper bills.

I made a list of organizations to notify that I no longer wanted to receive mailings. Then, I followed through and unsubscribed, either switching to electronic newsletters or bills or asking to be taken off the mailing list entirely.

Compostables

My city provides a large bin for organics that accepts yard trimmings, food waste, and all types of compostable packaging. Before dumping bags of food waste from the three-gallon container under my kitchen sink into the outdoor bin, I weighed them on the kitchen scale (I placed them in a bowl to keep the scale clean). I didn't weigh the yard trimmings, though. It wasn't practical and not important when considering waste streams to reduce.

Landfill

I separated two types of waste that go into the trash bin: used cat litter and trash from the cans around my house. I didn't want to weigh these on the kitchen scale for obvious reasons, so I used a bathroom scale and stepped on it while holding bags of trash. This method has a margin of error of at least half a pound compared to 0.1 ounces for the kitchen scale, but I decided that it was close enough.

The results of my waste tracking experiment showed that my household generated an average of 0.77 pounds of waste per person per day. That amount includes recycling, trash, and food waste for composting. You can see my detailed data on page 104.

I'm sharing my household's data at some risk. While my numbers are well below the US average, there will be those who claim that we still create too much waste given that I've been researching and writing about this topic for the past few years. My family has room for improvement. But by sharing data that isn't perfect, I hope that I can encourage others to do the same. If I had tracked our household waste prior to 2014, I expect that the numbers would have been much higher.

Here are some of the habits my family has incorporated in the past few years:

- Composting all food waste (moving to a city with curbside composting made that an obvious choice)
- Storing all leftovers in reusable containers
- Writing the date on all open containers to reduce food waste, and paying attention to those dates
- Reusing plastic bags from grocery store products to store food or dispose of cat litter
- Using beeswax wraps instead of plastic wrap
- Ordering produce that comes unwrapped in a cardboard box
- Bringing a reusable water bottle with me (when I forget, I try to find a drinking fountain instead of buying bottled water)
- Bringing a reusable cup to coffee shops

> Keeping fabric tote bags in my car for shopping

> Refilling my own containers in the bulk aisle of grocery stores

Some of these changes confused my family members, like when they asked why the cheddar cheese was inside a tortilla bag. It made sense to me. The tortillas that my family prefers are only sold in zip-top bags, I no longer buy plastic zipper baggies, and cheese dries out in beeswax wraps.

Most of my family's waste to landfill is cat litter. We're keeping the cat because he's part of the family (although I didn't count him as a member of the household for the purposes of calculating per capita waste). I've read that composting pet waste in the backyard is possible if you keep it separate, let it degrade for at least two years, and don't use the resulting compost for any edible crops.[1] But I think the project is too ambitious for us. It will probably be easier to convince my husband to remember to bring reusable bags to the grocery store and to buy fewer frozen meals.

Feel free to adopt any of my habits or choose different ones that work for you. Tracking your data will help you uncover gaps that you can view as opportunities for improvement. Implementing SMART goals (page 84) will help you follow through on reducing your household waste.

If reducing your annual waste to landfill to fit into a small trash can is not realistic for your family, you don't need to feel guilty. Your efforts to reduce waste do matter. We don't need a hundred families in the US achieving zero waste. We need millions of families in the US achieving more modest waste reduction goals and encouraging their friends and neighbors to do the same.

DO OUR EFFORTS MAKE A DIFFERENCE?

When I conduct waste reduction workshops, people sometimes ask what we can do about industrial waste. It is a fair question. The mining, manufacturing, oil and gas, and agriculture industries are the biggest contributors to industrial waste and are responsible for far more waste than the 130 million households in the US. The oft-quoted statistic saying that household waste only comprises 3% of total waste generation in the US is probably in the ballpark, but there's a lot of uncertainty because hard data is lacking.[2]

What can we do as citizens? We can ask the government and the EPA for better data and support regulations that encourage certain industries to reduce their waste footprint. Our requests may or may not result in change. Acting individually to manage our household waste, however, is something that will have a result, however small.

I don't have any illusion that smarter recycling is the solution to our country's waste problems or that it will do much to address climate change. But recycling is one piece of the puzzle. It costs nothing in money and not much in time. I've found over the past few years that I'm naturally shifting my behavior and questioning how much disposable stuff I'm using and what I'm doing with it. Millions of us doing the same can make a difference.

Our society needs to reduce the use of disposable packaging. Many industries need to get on board: food and beverage, health and beauty, consumer electronics, and more. Fortunately, momentum is building. As customers, we can vote with our dollars in choosing what to buy and what to avoid. If we all choose less wasteful but possibly a bit more expensive options, higher volume sales should eventually cause prices to come down.

In some cases, higher initial costs are balanced by lower ongoing costs because items need replacing less frequently. This long-term thinking is a way to see that many environmentally friendly choices are also economical.

We can evaluate marketing claims that say a product is eco-friendly and decide whether to believe them. How transparent does the company appear? I'll admit that it can be hard to tell. I don't expect most people to spend hours researching a company before deciding whether to buy its products. But I hope that I can inspire my readers to think harder and make one change at a time.

One change often leads to another. If you stop tossing plastic grocery bags into the recycling bin, it will force you to think about how many plastic bags you are using. Not only will you stop being part of the problem of plastic bags clogging the recycling equipment, you may choose to reduce your consumption of bags even if local laws do not force you to do so. Once you change your thinking about plastic bags, you will probably also consider other types of household waste.

You can also think beyond your household. If you work at an office, you can talk to your employer about reducing the use of disposable paper and plastic or labeling trash and recycling bins more clearly. If you organize community events, you can put out labeled bins for sorting and disposal, provide reusable or compostable plates and flatware, buy less food and find a place to donate or compost leftovers, and buy in bulk to avoid individual packaging (if public health guidelines allow that).

If you haven't yet completed the tracking worksheets in this chapter, I encourage you to do so. I also encourage you to fill in the SMART goals form. Each goal that you commit to may seem small, but it is a step forward.

Tracking Waste by Volume

For each recycling bin, note the type of recycling it accepts. Note the capacity of all bins in gallons.

Recycling bin 1: _____

Capacity: _____

Date started	Date filled	Days to fill

Gallons per day: _____

Garbage bin: _____

Capacity: _____

Date started	Date filled	Days to fill

Gallons per day: _____

Recycling bin 2: _____

Capacity: _____

Date started	Date filled	Days to fill

Gallons per day: _____

Yard Waste bin: _____

Capacity: _____

Date started	Date filled	Days to fill

Gallons per day: _____

Recycling bin 3: _____

Capacity: _____

Date started	Date filled	Days to fill

Gallons per day: _____

To calculate gallons per day, take the bin capacity in gallons and divide by the average number of days to fill.

Tracking Waste by Weight

Date range: _____

Recyclable paper:

Date	Weight, oz

Total (lb.) _____

Recyclable plastic:

Date	Weight, oz

Total (lb.) _____

Recyclable glass:

Date	Weight, oz

Total (lb.) _____

Recyclable metal:

Date	Weight, oz

Total (lb.) _____

Food waste for compost:

Date	Weight, oz

Total (lb.) _____

Trash for landfill:

Date	Weight, oz

Total (lb.) _____
Household size: _____
Weight/person/day

Grand total weight:_____
Household size:_____
Weight/person/day: _____

Notes: _____

_____

Tracking Waste by Counting

Date range: _____

RECYCLABLE PACKAGING

Item description	Tally of items	Total	Notes
Glass bottles			
Glass jars			
Metal cans			
Paper towel and TP tubes			
Paper-based food containers			
Plastic bottles, recyclable			
Plastic film (cling wrap)			
Plastic grocery bags			
Plastic jars			
Plastic tubs			

NON-RECYCLABLE TRASH OR HARD-TO-RECYCLE PACKAGING

Item description

Plastic food containers			
Padded mailing envelopes			
Styrofoam food containers			
Toothpaste tubes			

Tracking Waste by Counting

Date range: _____

RECYCLABLE PACKAGING

Item description	Tally of items	Total	Notes

NON-RECYCLABLE TRASH OR HARD-TO-RECYCLE PACKAGING

SMART Goals for Reducing Waste

Goal #:

S   Specific: what type of waste, how you will reduce it

_____

_____

M   Measurable: the numbers behind your goal

_____

_____

A   Achievable: potential barriers and ways to overcome them

_____

_____

R   Relevant: the reason behind this particular goal

_____

_____

T   Time-based: set a deadline for completion or a regular schedule

_____

_____

Goal #:

S   Specific: what type of waste, how you will reduce it

_____

_____

M   Measurable: the numbers behind your goal

_____

_____

A   Achievable: potential barriers and ways to overcome them

_____

_____

R   Relevant: the reason behind this particular goal

_____

_____

T   Time-based: set a deadline for completion or a regular schedule

_____

_____

To add more goals, download this worksheet at https://juliagoldsteinauthor.com/worksheets.

MAY 2020

My reusable coffee cups now sit unused in a cabinet in my kitchen. I no longer frequent coffee shops. I order coffee beans shipped to my house and brew my daily cup in my kitchen. My home office is just a few steps away.

The story I told at the beginning of this book happened many months ago, in a world when hanging out at coffee shops was commonplace and many freelancers and business owners favored co-working spaces. As I write this, cities are tentatively starting to allow nonessential businesses and small gatherings after the coronavirus (COVID-19) shutdown. Starbucks has reopened stores that were closed or only open for drive-through, but the indoor tables are still empty, and customers are not allowed to bring in reusable cups for sanitary reasons. In a blog post I wrote in March, I worried about the shift away from reusables just when awareness about the problems of disposable packaging was reaching a tipping point.

By the time you read this, America may have reopened all sorts of businesses, or the country may be experiencing more shutdowns as a second wave of the virus hits. Regardless how things progress, I believe that some practices will change permanently.

There is a new awareness around sanitizing everything from coffee mugs to countertops. With increased cleaning has come increased waste: disposable wipes, gloves, and masks are everywhere. Some are disposed of conscientiously, such as in drop boxes at office supply stores, while others are dropped carelessly in parking lots. Greater demand for online ordering has resulted in growing piles of cardboard boxes and plastic bubble wrap. Orders for takeout or delivery from restaurants come with plastic bags and forks. At least some services offer the option to decline napkins and plasticware.

It is vital to protect public health, but there is still a place for reusable items. We can wash cloth masks or sanitize them by leaving them out in the sun. Even at the height of the shutdown, I discovered that grocery stores allowed me to bring in cloth bags if I bagged my own groceries. After a few trips to the store, I got more efficient at bagging while developing a new appreciation for the workers who bag groceries all day long.

I hope that, rather than rely on bottled water, more people will develop the habit of bringing a reusable water bottle with them when they go out. If we feel that we can't safely drink from public water fountains, we may be more inclined to plan ahead. Perhaps traditional fountains will be increasingly replaced by bottle refill stations. Some models even show a digital readout of how many bottles they've refilled. They offer a visual reminder about avoiding the manufacturing, filling, shipping, and recycling or trashing of disposable bottles.

But there is still a need for smart recycling. If we can't take empty containers to stores and refill them from the bulk aisle, we can reuse them at home until they no longer function. If we rethink the bins, we can create cleaner waste streams that allow the essential work of waste hauling to be more efficient. We need community trash and recycling pickup to continue and can do our part by placing discarded items where they belong.

I wish you success in your journey toward a safer, less wasteful future.

Did you find this book useful? Please post a review so that other readers can discover it.

ACKNOWLEDGMENTS

Although I published my previous book, *Material Value*, with a business audience in mind, its message of cautious optimism and wealth of information appealed to readers beyond the business world. When I decided to write another book, I thought of those readers who appreciated the recycling chapter but wanted more practical tips. They inspired me to create this interactive guide.

This book came together quickly, thanks in part to research I completed in 2019 on a project for Xinova, one of my business clients. I wrote a report on the state of the waste disposal industry and some facts and figures I discovered while researching the report appear in the first chapter of this book.

I would like to thank my son, Dylan, for your enthusiastic participation when I tracked our household waste for a month to provide a concrete example. You have become much more aware of whether things are recyclable or compostable and keep looking for opportunities to reuse packaging.

When I reached out to my email list to announce my upcoming book project and request beta readers, they came through. My beta readers reviewed an early draft of the manuscript and also gave me feedback on titles and subtitles. Thanks to Andreas, Bruce, Christine, Diane, Francoise, Jessica, Stephen, and Polly for your valuable suggestions. You not only corrected minor errors but pointed out ways to better anticipate and answer readers' questions about waste and recycling.

Thanks to the team of professionals who transported this guide from a semi-polished manuscript to a finished book. Michelle, the cover is brilliant. You took my input on your original design concepts and ran with it. Sirajum, your creative infographics add so much more to the book than the dry Excel charts and diagrams I gave you. Ariel, thanks for pointing out places to add examples to make the concepts more real. It is great to have an editor who can take the reader's perspective and give me honest feedback. Abbey, I appreciate the extra set of keen eyes to spot errors and fix those pesky commas. Judi, your detailed index helps readers and makes the book more valuable to librarians.

Thanks to my virtual assistant, Nancy, whose administrative and book marketing support will help my book reach more readers. Your organizational skills and dedication to making this book a success are so valuable. It's hard being a one-woman marketing team, but thanks to you, I don't have to do it alone.

ABOUT THE AUTHOR

Author photograph © Dan Devries

Julia L F Goldstein holds a PhD in materials science and started her career as an engineer before migrating to journalism in 2001. She now writes white papers and other content for companies manufacturing a wide variety of products. She especially likes to help her clients share stories about products or processes that reduce waste and save resources. Julia is the author of the award-winning book *Material Value: More Sustainable, Less Wasteful Manufacturing of Everything from Cell Phones to Cleaning Products.* She is active in her local writing community and leads the Seattle chapter of the Nonfiction Authors Association. When she's not writing, she enjoys playing flute and piccolo and participating in triathlons.

Connect with the author: juliagoldsteinauthor.com

Follow her on Twitter:@jlfgoldstein

Did you enjoy this book? Please post a review to spread the word and help more readers discover it.

RESOURCES

My data tracking results

I am sharing the results of my tracking experiment in this book and I encourage you to share your tracking data with me. Go to https://julia-goldsteinauthor.com/submit to submit your results. The form accepts data from any of the three tracking methods that appear in Chapter 5. Once I receive enough responses, I will collate all the data and share it in aggregate.

As I mentioned in Chapter 5, I tracked my waste by weight. In one month, my household of three people generated 69.1 pounds of waste. We deposited the following into our recycling bin:

- 16.6 pounds of paper

- 1.2 pounds of plastic

- 8.0 pounds of glass

- 0.9 pounds of metal

We also collected 0.6 pounds of plastic bags for drop-off at the grocery store.

We deposited six bags of food waste totaling 15.8 pounds into the yard waste bin for composting and filled our garbage can with 26 pounds of trash. Most of the trash (21.5 pounds) was cat litter. This last result shouldn't have surprised me, because I know that the cat trash is heavy, but I didn't realize that it made up that much of our waste to landfill.

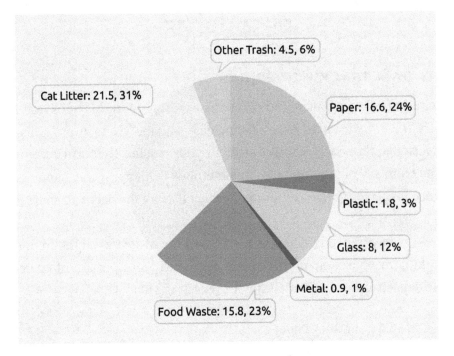

My household waste tracking data
Pounds generated during one month of data collection.

I used the tracking form that appears in this book and on my website. The calculations show that my household generated an average of 0.77 pounds of waste per person per day, 0.29 pounds of which went to landfill. While that total is well below the national average, my family is still going through more than 300 pounds per year of disposable stuff that can't be recycled or composted. There is room for improvement.

USEFUL BOOKS, REPORTS, AND WEBSITES

➤ Books for further reading

Dillehay, James. *Start a Creative Recycling Side Hustle: 101 Ideas for Making Money from Sustainable Crafts Consumers Crave.* Torreon, NM: Warm Snow Publishers, 2020.

Freinkel, Susan. *Plastic: A Toxic Love Story.* New York: Houghton Mifflin, 2011.

Gershuny, Grace. *The Rodale Book of Composting: Easy Methods for Every Gardener.* New York: Rodale Books, 1992.

Humes, Edward. *Garbology: Our Dirty Love Affair with Trash.* New York: Avery, 2012.

Johnson, Bea. *Zero Waste Home: The Ultimate Guide to Simplifying Your Life by Reducing Your Waste.* New York: Scribner, 2013.

Kellogg, Kathryn. *101 Ways to Go Zero Waste.* New York: The Countryman Press, 2019.

Lightner, Jill. *Scraps, Peels, and Stems: Recipes and Tips for Rethinking Food Waste at Home.* Seattle: Skipstone, 2018.

Liu, Christine. *Sustainable Home: Practical Projects, Tips and Advice for Maintaining a More Eco-friendly Household.* London: White Lion Publishing, 2018.

Minter, Adam. *Junkyard Planet: Travels in the Billion-Dollar Trash Trade.* New York: Bloomsbury Publishing, 2013.

Minter, Adam. *Secondhand: Travels in the New Global Garage Sale.* New York: Bloomsbury Publishing, 2019.

Terry, Beth. *Plastic Free: How I Kicked the Plastic Habit and How You Can Too.* New York: Skyhorse Publishing, 2013.

SanClements, Michael. *Plastic Purge: How to Use Less Plastic, Eat Better, Keep Toxins Out of Your Body, and Help Save the Sea Turtles!* New York: St. Martin's Griffin, 2014.

Szaky, Tom. *The Future of Packaging: From Linear to Circular.* Oakland, CA: Berrett-Koehler Publishers, Inc., 2019.

➤ Composting resources

The American Horticultural Society's Master Gardeners program, https://www.ahsgardening.org/gardening-resources/master-gardeners

USDA Agricultural Research Service (search for "compost"), https://www.ars.usda.gov

➤ Curbside pickup or mailing of hard-to-recycle items

Loop (Eastern US), https://loopstore.com

Retrievr (New Jersey and Pennsylvania), https://retrievr.com)

Ridwell (Seattle area), https://www.ridwell.com

Terracycle (availability varies by program), https://www.terracycle.com/en-US

➤ Major waste hauling and processing companies in North America

(service is available through at least one of these companies in every US state but not necessarily every community)

Waste Management, Inc., https://www.wm.com/us/en/myhome

Republic Services, https://www.republicservices.com

Waste Connections, Inc., https://www.wasteconnections.com

Strategic Materials, https://www.strategicmaterials.com

➤ Organizations accepting used consumer electronics

Cell Phones for Soldiers, https://www.cellphonesforsoldiers.com

Medic Mobile, https://medicmobile.org/phone-donations

National Coalition Against Domestic Violence, https://ncadv.org/donate-a-phone

Secure the Call, https://securethecall.org/how-we-do-it

➤ Recycling options look-up

Earth 911, resource for many types of materials (nationwide), https://www.earth911.com

Hazardous waste handling, https://hazwastehelp.org (King County, Washington state)

➤ Resources for selling scrap metal

iScrap App (smartphone app), https://iscrapapp.com

➤ Tools for calculating waste

Greenpeace UK plastics calculator, https://secure.greenpeace.org.uk/page/content/plastics-calculator

My Little Plastic Footprint (smartphone app), https://mylittleplastic-footprint.org

Omni Calculator, https://www.omnicalculator.com/ecology/plastic-footprint

➤ Websites for further research

"The Circular Economy," The Ellen MacArthur Foundation, accessed 10 June 2020, https://www.ellenmacarthurfoundation.org/circular-economy/what-is-the-circular-economy.

NOTES

Chapter 1:

1. "Advancing Sustainable Materials Management: 2017 Fact Sheet." US Environmental Protection Agency, published November 2019, https://www.epa.gov/sites/production/files/2019-11/documents/2017_facts_and_figures_fact_sheet_final.pdf.

2. Edward Humes, *Garbology: Our Dirty Love Affair with Trash* (New York: Penguin, 2012), 256.

3. Jan Dell, "U.S. Plastic Recycling Rate Projected to Drop to 4.4% in 2018," *The Plastic Pollution Coalition*, 4 October 2018. https://www.plasticpollutioncoalition.org/blog/2018/10/4/us-plastic-recycling-rate-projected-to-drop-to-44-in-2018.

4. Scott Mouw, et al., "2020 State of Curbside Recycling Report," *The Recycling Partnership*, 13 February 2020.

5. Abi Bradford, Sylvia Broude, and Alexander Truelove, *Trash in America: Moving from Destructive Consumption to a Zero-Waste System* (U.S. PIRG Education Fund, February 2018), 14.

6. "Composting in America," U.S. PIRG Education Fund and Frontier Group, 13 June 2019. https://uspirg.org/reports/usp/composting-america.

7. *Project and Landfill Data by State*, US Environmental Protection Agency, modified July 2019, accessed 17 Oct 2019, https://www.epa.gov/lmop/project-and-landfill-data-state.

8. "Refrigerant management," Project Drawdown (website), accessed 10 June 2020, https://www.drawdown.org/solutions/materials/refrigerant-management.

9. Mouw, "2020 State of Curbside Recycling Report."

Chapter 3:

1. Humes, *Garbology,* 144.

2. Virginia Streeter and Brenda Platt, "Residential Food Waste Collection Access in The U.S.," *BioCycle*, 58(11), December 2017.

3. "National overview: facts and figures on materials, wastes and recycling," US Environmental Protection Agency, modified March 13, 2020, https://www.epa.gov/facts-and-figures-about-materials-waste-and-recycling/national-overview-facts-and-figures-materials#Recycling/Composting.

4. Erin McCoy, "Where does all the trash from Dollywood go? To one of the world's best composting facilities," *Yes! Magazine*, August 28, 2014, https://www.yesmagazine.org/environment/2014/08/28/sevier-county-composting/

Chapter 4:

1. A. J. Bradford, *Composting in America: A Path to Eliminate Waste, Revitalize Soil and Tackle Global Warming.* U.S. PIRG and Frontier Group, 2019.

2. "Solutions," Project Drawdown (website), accessed 10 June 2020, https://www.drawdown.org/solutions

3. Streeter, "Residential Food Waste."

4. Claire Thompson, "Paper, Plastic or Reusable?" *Stanford Magazine*, last modified September 2017, https://stanfordmag.org/contents/paper-plastic-or-reusable.

5. "Glass Clean-up Systems in MRFs", Closed Loop Foundation (website), published 25 Sept 2019, http://www.closedlooppartners.com/wp-content/uploads/2017/04/20170419_CLFdn-Glass-Study_Final_Public.pdf.

6. "All States Table," Bottle Bill Resource Guide (website), accessed 10 June 2020, http://www.bottlebill.org/index.php/current-and-proposed-laws/usa/additional-links.

7. "Map of States With Legislation," Electronics Recycling Coordination Clearinghouse, accessed 10 June 2020, https://www.ecycle-clearinghouse.org/contentpage.aspx?pageid=10.

8. "UN report: Time to seize opportunity, tackle challenge of e-waste," United Nations Environment Programme, published 24 January 2019, https://www.unenvironment. org/news-and-stories/press-release/un-report-time-seize-opportunity-tackle-challenge-e-waste.

Chapter 5:

1. Colleen Vanderlinden, "How to compost pet waste," *thespruce. com*, last updated January 17, 2020, https://www.thespruce.com/composting-cat-or-dog-waste-2539613.

2. Max Liboiron, "Municipal versus Industrial Waste: Questioning the 3-97 ratio," Discard Studies, publication date March 2, 2016, https://discardstudies.com/2016/03/02/municipal-versus-industrial-waste-a-3-97-ratio-or-something-else-entirely/.

INDEX

Page numbers with an *f* refer to a figure.

CPSIA information can be obtained
at www.ICGtesting.com
Printed in the USA
LVHW011643120121
676309LV00016B/2259

9 780999 595640